the Jew and the Other

the Jew and the Other

Esther Benbassa and Jean-Christophe Attias

translated from the French by G. M. Goshgarian

CORNELL UNIVERSITY PRESS   ITHACA AND LONDON

Originally published in 2002 by Editions du Relié as *Le Juif et l'autre*, by Esther Benbassa and Jean-Christophe Attias. Copyright © Le Relié, 2002.

This translation was prepared with the generous assistance of the French Ministry of Culture—Ouvrage publié avec le concours du Ministère français chargé de la Culture—Centre national du Livre.

First Published 2004 by Cornell University Press
First printing, Cornell Paperbacks, 2003

Printed in the United States of America

Library of Congress Cataloging-in-Publication Data

Benbassa, Esther.
    [Juif et l'autre. English]
    The Jew and the other / Esther Benbassa and Jean-Christophe Attias ; translated from the French by G. M. Goshgarian.
        p. cm.
    Includes bibliographical references and index.
    ISBN 0-8014-4247-8 (cloth : alk. paper) — ISBN 0-8014-8946-6 (pbk. : alk. paper)
    1. Judaism—Essence, genius, nature. 2. Jews—Identity.
I. Attias, Jean-Christophe. II. Title.
    BM565.B4413 2004
    296—dc22

                                                    2004010508

Cornell University Press strives to use environmentally responsible suppliers and materials to the fullest extent possible in the publishing of its book. Such materials include vegetable-based, low-VOC inks and acid-free papers that are recycled, totally chlorine-free, or partly composed of nonwood fibers. For further information, visit our website at www.cornellpress.cornell.edu.

Cloth printing   10   9   8   7   6   5   4   3   2   1
Paperback printing 10   9   8   7   6   5   4   3   2   1

*T*here have always been in Judaism, from time immemorial, two strains grappling with each other in a duel. One is the isolationist. It hates the stranger, fosters the Amalek complex, and at every opportunity emphasizes "Remember what they did to you." and there is another Judaism, which I would characterize perhaps with the verse "Love thy neighbor as thyself." This is a Judaism whose prayer is, "Allow me to forget Amalek"—a Judaism of love and forgiveness.

—Samuel Hugo Bergman (1883–1975)

Contents

Introduction

In memory of Robert Attias

In the West, the Jew is the other. He is an intimate other, in some sort. He is such, to begin with, thanks to the continuous presence on the European continent of Jewish communities that have, in some cases, displayed an astonishing stability for hundreds of years. He is such, again, because European civilization has to some extent constructed itself by contemplating its reflection in him. The Jew is the other from which triumphant Christianity emerged, and, simultaneously, in opposition to which it has become what it is. He is an intimate, lastly, because it was in following the sometimes convoluted yet decisive paths of emancipation and integration that the Western Jew fully assumed his role in the advent and development of modernity in the contemporary period, on both sides of the Atlantic. Compounded of rejection and, in equal measure, fascination, of envy but also admiration, the gaze that the West has brought to bear on the Jew as other has also had a great deal to do with fashioning the gaze that the Jew has brought to bear on himself.

The fact remains, however, that the Jew is not simply the West's other. Nor is he simply what he has finally become today, the other of a certain Islam. The Jew is a subject. And, like all human societies, Jewish society too has relied on the image of the other in constructing and defining itself. It has made use of the non-Jewish other and the Jewish other as well. In their fashion, the untold recastings and remodelings of this image bear witness to the mutations and the profound mutability, throughout history, of Jewish identity itself. Ask the Jews how they conceive of the other and you will soon learn how they conceive of themselves. The ambiguousness of the figure of the other as a socio-cultural construct reflects the ambiguousness of the one who produces it. The reason is that the other is also always another self: a mirror and, at the same time, a foil. This is doubtless a rather widely applicable truth. Yet it may well apply the more powerfully to a group that has historically been a dispersed minority, and therefore been vulnerable and naturally inclined to feel both attracted and threatened by the majority in the society in which it lives.

Such is the shifting ground that we have set out to explore in the following essay. It is, doubtless, natural that this exploration should proceed in five stages, moving in step, as it were, with another Book, the Bible, pausing over one or another of its verses and endlessly ringing change after change on them, like some improbable modern *midrash*.[1]

For what is the Pentateuch, after all? It is the text around which the Jewish community has come together, the text with which it identifies and which it puts at the heart of its liturgy. The ritual ensures that it will be read chapter by chapter, week by week. This reading ends when the year does. It can then start over again "from the beginning"—and so on, indefinitely. Thus the Pentateuch is a text for internal consumption, one whose interminable spiral envelops and protects the group. But it is also the text of the other. It makes up the core of the Old Testament appropriated by a Christianity that has chosen to regard it as an embryonic form, but only an embryonic form, of a message the keys to which are all to be found in the New.

What else is the Pentateuch? It is Moses' written record of the word of the wholly-other, of a God who, in some sense, invents the people of Israel the moment he makes a covenant with it. It is, with Adam and Noah, the history of the beginnings of humanity and, with Abraham, of the beginnings of a people unlike all the others. It is an account of the tribulations that gradually allowed this people to tear itself from the indistinction of the merely human, divorce itself from the other, and take on its own identity in the act of breaking with every imaginable Egypt and every sort of slavery. It is, finally, the text of the Law that justifies and codifies the distinction between the permitted and the forbidden, and between self and other.

Yet the Pentateuch is simultaneously the narrative of something left unfinished, because everything comes to a halt on the threshold of the Promised Land, and because Moses himself, the spokesman and secretary of the Lord, dies in the wilderness, not quite sure, perhaps, that he has fully accomplished his task, and cheated, in any case, of all the future achievements in which he is by no means invited to take part. The Law of the Pentateuch is not an iron Law and it is hardly unambiguous. In this Law, the demand for separation rubs shoulders with the ethical demand: the other is a temptation and a danger, but he is also an object of compassion and the beneficiary of a genuinely even-handed justice.

Finally, the Pentateuch is a text that has, like some impregnable fortress, withstood the onslaughts of countless generations of commentators. It is an obscure, contradictory, sometimes shocking text, one that, albeit well and truly ours, has nevertheless also shown itself to be cruelly other. Century after century, it has had critics sweating blood and tears in the effort to re-appropriate it, to turn its words every which way in order to tease new, intelligible, acceptable meanings out of them. It has invited both ancient and modern thinkers to display the kind of hermeneutic daring which alone can save it.

We need only think of our contemporaries. Humanist, universalistic Jewish thinkers have staunchly resisted the temptation of a narrow particularism without therefore abandoning the principle of Election—that is, of the singularity and value of the Jewish experience. Jewish feminists have confronted the "male chauvinism" of this text. Even Jewish gays have tried to limit or neutralize its "homophobia." What, indeed, are we to make, today, of a text that a secularized Jewish nationalism has transformed into a political charter and the basis for a historical claim? What are we to make of a text that, in both its history of the Creation and its enunciation of the Law, puts women in a position of subjection and subordination? What are we to do with a text that imposes the death penalty on what it regards as the "abomination" of sexual relations between two men?

However, at bottom, the Bible is of no significance whatsoever. What counts is its readers: those flesh-and-blood Jews, past and present, who have sought to open, in the wall of its discourse, the breach through which the other can slip once again, and through which life can once again flow in order to irrigate the aridity of this text and re-animate words grown stiff and brittle with age. The other is still a part of this text, because, like it or not, the other is still a part of life. He who seeks it there shall find it there. And, finding it, he shall find himself. Indeed, the figure of the other, whether mirror or foil, always emerges amidst ambiguity, because that figure is emblematic of an ultimate, irreducible interdependence, and because it is ultimately the other who makes me what I am and allows me fully to realize myself. Ultimately, the self is never possible without the other. The Book needs its readers. The text needs life. And the Jew needs his other. Let us, then, interrogate this text, fecundating it with the lessons of history—in other words, of life. In the (his)story it tells, there is something not just for the Jew, but for his other as well.

Collegium Budapest, June 2002

the Jew and the Other

1 Genesis

The Divine, the Human, the Feminine

Leave your own country, your kin, and your father's house, and go to a country which I will show you.

—Genesis 12:1

The Eternal here orders Abraham to go into exile. That is the price he must pay in order to found a great nation and cover his name with glory. Blessing will be his reward. So, at the age of seventy-five, the patriarch leaves Chaldea, the land of his ancestors, for the land of Canaan, the country the Eternal has promised to his descendants. This is where the odyssey of the Jewish people begins. The history of the Jews has its roots in a departure and their covenant is sealed in a foreign country. To be Jewish is in fact a way of being other: other than what one is. It is a way of being from elsewhere and going elsewhere, as part of the constantly reaffirmed project of encountering the other. It is the otherness of a new land and the otherness of an old one as well. It is a strangely originary otherness that one never ceases to carry within oneself, at the very core of one's relation to oneself. For the encounter with the other is proof not only of adaptation but also of identification. And it is also in one's relation to the most intimate of others, and with him, that one elaborates one's identity and constructs one's particularity.

Thus the people descended of Abraham arrived in Canaan from outside it, as other, and gradually moved, as the conquest proceeded, from periphery to center. The future people of Israel settled on this foreign territory. Yahweh himself is a foreigner in this country, for he "came from Sinai,"[2] a remote place at the heart of the wilderness. The tribes of Israel made their way into the land promised to their ancestors, but it was in no sense a land of which they were the native inhabitants. It was their adopted land, a land that they gradually conquered and where they collided with others, its inhabitants, the Philistines and Canaanites. The Bible makes the Philistines the implacable enemies of the Israelites: it regards them as an idolatrous people and holds their gods up to ridicule. It describes the Canaanites as the country's original inhabitants, its true natives. They are the closest, most intimate other: their ancient presence on this soil endows them with a legitimacy that the Philistines lack. This most intimate other is not lacking in positive qualities, but it is depraved. The conquest, as a result, becomes a moral act.

The myth, of course, has it that all Israel is descended of Abraham and Sarah. Yet the other is not absent from this genealogy. It is everywhere, adulterating this supposed purity. The people of Israel is not a simple family, nor is it simply a family. It is constructed in an encounter with the other nations. Its monotheism is elaborated in this confrontation with the idolatrous peoples and the conquest is invested with meaning on condition that the temptation they represent is resisted. Were Abraham's ancestors not themselves pagans? The other lies in wait for the nascent Hebrew people, rendering it vulnerable while at the same time inspiring it with the strength that it needs in order to be and to situate itself. The moral and religious particularity of the Israelites distinguishes them from the surrounding peoples. It authorizes and legitimizes their identity. It is true that they were once idolaters, but they no longer shall be, because their hosts still are. The others trace the cultural frontiers of the people of Israel, and the borderline they draw both singularizes the Israelites and rivets them to this foreign soil. It creates the solidarity that is indispensable for a people in movement; the looks exchanged between them and the others contribute to their self-understanding. The rejection of the other that is constitutive of the collective religious and national identity presupposes, at the outset, the greatest imaginable proximity. In order to come about, it has no choice but to leave this other behind, without, however, losing track of it. At every step of the way, the Jew and the other are bound up with each other and separated from each other, seek each other and abandon each other. But neither ever forgets the other.

Abraham's posterity goes into exile in Egypt in order to escape the famine and poverty rampant in Canaan. Moses, the nation's future lawgiver, is born on this foreign soil, and it is on this foreign soil that the house of Jacob increases and multiplies. Brought up by Pharaoh's daughter, Moses incontestably bears within him the otherness from which it is his mission to free Israel. In the modern and contemporary periods, some would even entertain the illusion that he was purely and simply of Egyptian birth. In any event, the Promised Land remains forever foreign to him; Moses never sets foot on the soil of Canaan. He leads the Hebrews out of Egypt, transmits the Torah to them, and accompanies them during their forty years of wandering in the wilderness, a neutral territory from which the other, like the self, is absent. And he dies on the eve of their arrival in this land blessed by God.

Unmistakably foreign, Moses would never cease to fascinate the Jews on their long diasporic journey. The modern artists and thinkers who were torn between a desire for integration—a wish to live like their compatriots in countries of adoption that were also, for many of them, their native countries—and their ties to the ancient people from which they were descended, could not but identify with their illustrious predecessor. The emblematic figure of Moses haunted Freud, Kafka, Heine, and Schönberg at the end of their lives, lives that were all journeys of torment, interrogation, and exile. It was in exile that Freud, who had become an undesirable alien in his native city and the land of his birth, wrote his *Moses and Monotheism*. It was in telling the story of this other, Moses, that he wrote his own "family romance." Both Heine, a convert to Christianity, and Schönberg, another convert, had become other from the standpoint of Judaism; yet both sought consolation in the profoundly moral figure of this Hebrew of Egyptian birth. Moses' inner exile is also that of a Kafka. And it is that of untold other Jews undergoing the wrenching experience of integration or assimilation—of full-fledged entry into the other's world, which, however, never stops rejecting them, despite all their efforts to resemble the other as closely as they can. In nineteenth-century central Europe, the destiny of these tormented intellectuals could not but intersect that of Moses, who, like them, was also often betrayed by his own people.

Members of a minority in the countries in which they live, the Jews cannot imagine themselves without the other; yet they are forever caught up in a dual relation of rejection and attraction, one they experience daily. If they are rejected, they are tempted to reject the other in their turn, maintaining their singularity by any means available, refusing to melt and disappear. Yet the other is unavoidable. Jewish identity is woven of repulsion and fascination, the Jew's and the other's. The Jews need the other. It is through him that they open themselves up to the world and to themselves, reaping, one by one, the advantages of a founding act that brings them face-to-face with their neighbor, so different from, and, at the same time, so much like them.

The vicissitudes of history have certainly helped to reinforce an attitude of reserve. Modern anti-Semitism has cast the Jew himself as definitely, absolutely, irreducibly other. In the anti-Semite's eyes, the Jew is not distinguished from the non-Jew by his religion alone, a religion that, moreover, he usually does not practice. He is not merely a second-class citizen or subject. He becomes the other par excellence, the racially other, and is considered irremediably inferior, even if he is also infinitely dangerous. The Jew is the intimate enemy, an enemy who must be struck down. This is no longer the diabolical Jew of the Middle Ages. It is a Jew who cannot now be recognized as a Jew, because he is culturally and socially integrated or even assimilated. Yet he is imagined to be, despite appearances, fundamentally other, even if he himself thinks that he is more like the others than ever before.

So much like the others, or trying so hard to be like them, this Jew devotes himself to working wholeheartedly for the welfare of his fellows with a view to creating the harmony that they so sorely need. From anarchism to Marxism, he participates in the full range of modern movements. He merges with the other for the other's sake in order to abolish borders and bring a redeemed, just, equitable world into being. In the new order that he hopes to build in communion with the other, by fighting alongside him, he sets *himself* up as an other responsible for all the ills, wars, and upheavals that have beset mankind for the past two centuries. He throws himself body and soul into the future. He makes a commitment to modernity in order to guarantee—with the other, always— the progress that he expects will bring happiness. When he is not a revolutionary, he invests in industry, banking, the railways, and all the other attributes of a modernity that puts him at the forefront of things. Are progress and creation not forms of collective writing? Do they not imply that everyone must participate in the moving, changing world of the living? But, here too, the Jew inspires fear. His enemies are afraid that they will not be able to keep pace with the new course of things and therefore reject the Jew and modernity at the same time, conflating the one with the other.

Yet, down to the gaze that he turns on others, whether they reject, ignore, or acknowledge him— down to the image in which, in novels, films, or the arts, he mirrors the society in which he takes an active part—the Jew is still the one who enlightens this society about itself, thanks to the miracle of his proximity to it and the distance that he simultaneously knows how to keep from it. Jewish writers, filmmakers, and painters shed light on themselves even as they shed light on the world; they are themselves creators of places without borders that are also places of hospitality, in which, for the space of an instant, the gap between "us" and "the others" disappears. They sow confusion in order to bring out that difference in the absence of which dialogue with the other runs dry in the desert of absence.

Will it be said that the Jews are all alike, if only physically? The Jews carry their country on their backs, and bear its marks. They negotiate reality in their languages, which are peculiar to them and, at the same time, something they have in common with the rest of the human race. They are both in and of the world. Although a minority, they are encouraged to share—to share cultures, gestures, manners, ways of looking at things—and to take from others things that eventually become natural for them too, a part of their very being.

Will it be objected that the Jew is a cosmopolitan? Is this because he is different, or because he takes from the world what the world owes him, because the world is his world? Is it exile that has made him so permeable? Even after he has ceased to be a cosmopolitan, and, having gone back to the land that God once promised him, counts it as his duty to cease to be one—even today, in the modern state of Israel, the Jew carries his land of origin in his baggage. Even those Jews who were born in Israel, the natives, the *sabras,* go back, if only for the space of a voyage or a pilgrimage, to the land in which their parents or ancestors lived. They feel an irresistible compulsion to (re)discover the elsewhere that will allow them to find themselves and seize hold of their very Israeliness [*is-raélité*]. It may be that, without the other, the Jew feels irrevocably alone: he is separated from himself as much as he is separated from a neighbor at once very similar and very different, who, when he is present, compels the Jew to be himself. Might it be that being Jewish is simply a way of being a man or a woman and that one can never be a man or a woman, and Jewish, in the absence of the other? Being Jewish would then mean just this: it would mean being a man or a woman like the others, with the others. It would mean cultivating awareness of a singularity, Jewishness, that creates distance while simultaneously, and even more profoundly, overcoming it. It would mean enjoying an experience that is both human and Jewish, transmissible and unique, an experience which is never fully realized and begins anew every day.

This experience is not—with all due respect to modern opinion—a strictly human affair. For, even if he is rejected, even if he is absent, and even if he is "dead," God, the wholly-other, has a hand in this business.

God created man in his image; in the divine image he created him.

—Genesis 1:27

At dawn, when he opens his eyes and tears himself from sleep, the practicing Jew thanks the Eternal for giving him back his soul or breath. For every awakening is a rebirth; it evokes the first moment in which God, in order to animate the creature whom he had made out of earth, blew the breath of life into his nostrils. Every awakening is an occasion to recall, in fear and thankfulness, the relationship that binds man to his Creator. For man, it is a relationship of permanent, radical dependence, and one of true intimacy as well, experienced from the moment he draws his first breath in the morning.

Doubtless God is by no means man. He is the other, the absolutely other. He is alive, powerful, and knowing. But he is not alive the way men are alive, or powerful the way men are powerful, or knowing the way men are knowing. Human language can only ever speak of him in approximate terms or by homonymy. He is eternally hidden, forever mysterious, inaccessible to the end of time. Yet it is this very God who creates the world and, in an act of unprecedented generosity, withdraws in order to make room for it. It is this same God who speaks to men, reveals his Law to them, rewards and chastens them. Thus the absolutely other is paradoxically present, close by, at the very heart of life. In his infinite wisdom, he desired his creature and desired to enter into a dialogue with him. He renounced the absolute character of his otherness and chose to turn his attentive, loving or wrathful regard on all that transpires here below. He chose to become a God to whom every man might address his prayers and to whom every Jew might give thanks—beginning in the morning, when he opens his eyes on the world that he brought into existence and maintains in its existence.

Thus the absolutely other is also man's fellow creature after all. It is in his image and likeness that man was created. Indeed, it is precisely this incredible kinship between the human and the divine that founds the ethical demand. Every blow struck against man is a blow struck against the image of God in man. Philosophers and mystics offer differing interpretations of the many kinds of anthropomorphism employed in the Bible, a discourse which, albeit divinely inspired, speaks the language of men in order to describe the divinity. Does God really have a body, an arm that he stretches forth, a mighty hand? Does he, then, have eyes with which to see and ears with which to hear? Does he have a mouth with which to make himself heard? How are such formulas to be understood? Are they allegories? Are they poetic evocations of infra-divine realities, angels and go-betweens?

The ambiguity is there, inscribed in the texts. Of all the prophets, Moses was doubtless the one who had the closest contact with God. Moses needed neither dreams nor visions in order to communicate with him. He spoke with him mouth to mouth, "face to face, as one man speaks to another."[3] Yet this extraordinary proximity had a limit that could never be crossed. Moses was never to see God's Face, but only his back, for man cannot see God "and still live."[4]

Insurmountable even for the first of the prophets, this ambiguousness of the Divine can be traced back to the combination of two different demands. One cannot humanize God without thereby de-deifying him. But a God that is too other, too distant, is a God who does not exist—not, at any rate, for men. God, however, needs men, and men themselves have to be able to experience their need for God. Communication presupposes community. God has to be able to serve men as a model; it has to be possible to imitate him. You will be holy, he says, because I am holy. Men have to be able to conclude a contract with him, to seal an alliance with him. Between the two allies or contracting parties, there has to be some sort of commensurability, even if it is limited in scope or infinitesimally small.

God does not make himself man, but multiple links are forged between him and men. With the consent of the hidden God, there appears a manifest God. The creation of the here below is only the final step in a long, complex process of emanation that makes it possible to conceive of the inconceivable passage from the One to the multiple in terms not just of rupture, but of continuity. Between God and this world, between God and man, there springs up a multifarious, mysterious universe. Angelic emissaries, columns of clouds and columns of fire, visible Glory, a burning bush, Ezechiel's chariot, a living, moving hierarchy of intermediate spheres, the *Sefirot* of the kabbalists. . . .[5] God inevitably finds himself drawn into the here below. Although he is invisible, and making images of him is forbidden, he has his House on a hill in Jerusalem. Although he contains this world, he is, at the same time, never absent from any place in the world. Although he is transcendent, he is also immanent in the feminine forms of a presence, the *Shekhinah*. One encounters him everywhere, in everything: in the wind that sets the mountains to quaking and shatters the rocks, in earthquakes and conflagrations, in the thin sound of silence. . . .

The Holy One, blessed be he, the God with the name that is never pronounced, is also the One to whom one calls out in distress, whom one calls upon as a witness in the face of iniquity, whom one celebrates in joy. He is close to everyone's heart; he raises up those who stumble; he visits the sick; he guides those who pass through the night. And he shares the emotions of those he loves. He weeps over the destruction of Jerusalem and goes into exile with his people. He is both just and merciful. He is capable of addressing a prayer to himself so that his compassion may prevail over his wrath. He studies the Law and wears phylacteries. He presides over a heavenly academy and himself teaches the Torah to Jewish children who have died prematurely.

And if God himself is not as close to man or as much like man as man might wish, many are those who, in the simplicity of everyday life as well as in the bitterness of great suffering, are capable of becoming his intermediaries—who are, to differing degrees, human bearers of the divine. There is Elijah, a prophet of the close-to-hand, a traveler or simple passerby who is capable of materializing at any moment in order to protect, warn, and announce. Or a holy miracle-worker, an intercessor in his lifetime but also after his death, whose tomb people will piously visit in hopes of receiving a blessing or being cured of some ill. Or, again, an erudite rabbi, a doctor and interpreter of the Law, a counselor to his charges and a guide for men of faith. . . .

God, then, is very close to man and very much like him. But that is just one of the experiences of the Divine. For the Divine makes itself felt in equal measure, and, no doubt, still more powerfully, in absence and separation—and in Evil.

For man, in whom God has implanted a powerful instinct for evil, is by no means the only one to discover that he is always irremediably other than himself, both in the suffering his fellows inflict upon him as well as in that he inflicts upon his fellows. No less than man, God too appears to be irremediably other than himself—and radically foreign to the world. The reason is precisely that he is one and that there is no other God but him; it is he who forms the light and creates the darkness, he who is the author of peace and woe. "I," says the Eternal, "do all these things."[6] There is "another side" to God, a baleful excess of force. God veils his Face, turns away from the world and withdraws from it. This withdrawal by itself suffices to authorize or bring about evil. Who is prepared to believe that nothing more is involved here than well-deserved punishment for an avowed crime? The suffering of the just and the good fortune of the evil confront the human mind with a question that will go forever unanswered. They force a difficult choice on it: either God does not exist or else he is so utterly other that no one can fathom his ways.

Job was a just man, "blameless and upright, who feared God and avoided evil."[7] Yet God smote him with sorrows, ruin, and "malignant ulcers from the soles of his feet to the crown of his head,"[8] confronting us with the unfathomable mystery of unmerited suffering. Job's complaint has never ceased. It finds a sinister echo in others, after him and like him. The principle of divine justice seems hopelessly compromised by the spectacle of a world delivered up to Evil and misfortune. Indeed, the history of the Jewish people is itself the subject of an abiding scandal. None of its transgressions seem to warrant, in human terms, the inordinate punishments that come raining down upon it: exile, persecution, massacre. From time to time, its tribulations incline it to make sacrifices or awaken its doubts.

For there exists a long Jewish tradition of adjurations addressed to Heaven, a long tradition of interrogations, quarrels, and struggles that goes all the way back to the patriarch Jacob and his combat with the Angel. The Jews call their God to account. Their rebelliousness is expressed in veiled terms or even openly. Apostasy itself is perhaps no more than this: it consists in abandoning a God who seems to have abandoned his people and to show no gratitude for its fidelity. Unbelief is perhaps nothing other than this: grieving over a world that God has abandoned.

Is the justification of God's ways that was invented by the rabbis not all too human? "The Holy One, blessed be he, inflicts suffering on the just in this world so that they may inherit the world to come . . . God confers an abundance of goods on the evil in this world in order to bring their souls to ruin and make certain that they will inherit the depths" of Hell.[9] Who, in the face of the horrors spawned by the century that has just ended or those that the already monstrous new one has begun to breed, will say, with the humility of Job, "I have dealt with great things that I do not understand; things too wonderful for me, which I cannot know"?[10] There is, perhaps, no other way to save God than to restore his absolute otherness.

Unless, that is, one should take precisely the opposite tack, re-humanizing him to the point of admitting his relative helplessness. This would make God one of the victims of Evil rather than its author. He would be a God who goes into exile with his people and, side-by-side with it, submits to the punishment that he inflicts upon it. . . . Man, the Jews, and God himself would thus all share the same exile: man driven from the Garden of Eden, the Jews driven from their lands, and, finally, the *Shekhinah,* the divine "Presence" or feminine part of the Lord, driven from her Temple and so cut off from her masculine principle. Do ancient rabbinical narratives not describe the sorrowful lamentation of the "Presence," the loving Mother of Israel, who covers the walls and columns of the Sanctuary with kisses and caresses and leaves it only reluctantly? Exile would accordingly mean this above all: the *Shekhinah* separated from her Temple, God separated from himself. A split in God, a split in man, with the fragility of the one echoing the fragility of the other. A violent cleavage, in God as well as in man, between the masculine and the feminine.

Male and female he created them.
—Genesis 1:27

For it is here, obviously, that we find the absolute, paradoxical experience of otherness in its root form: the strange confrontation of masculine and feminine; the recognition, in the other, of an irreducible difference but also an irreducible similarity; the awareness of a painful rupture and the longing for a lost harmony.

God, we are told, created man male and female at the same time. But we are also told just the opposite: that the male was created first, and that God then endowed him, because it was not good that he should be alone, with a "help-meet" taken from him, not directly from the earth. Of course, we are ultimately provided with an interpretation that reconciles the two halves of the original scenario: God in fact created an androgynous man, a man both male and female, and then divided him into a male on the one hand and a female on the other. Is woman man's other or simply man's other half? The nuance matters, to be sure, and has far-reaching implications. This holds, moreover, for God as well as man, because there is something feminine in God too, and because the aspiration for reunification or the harmonious reunion of the two principles is, precisely, the driving force behind human history, divine history, and the history of the world. Reunification, of course, will bring the end of exile for one and all. All will then "become one flesh."[11]

Judaism gives the impression of refusing to choose among these different approaches, and for good reason: Judaism is a man's affair. For centuries, only one Jewish voice succeeded in making itself heard, that of Jewish men. And that voice could never relinquish an image of woman as man's other, except when, in our own century, women themselves forced it to. Emmanuel Levinas, a Jewish man, also believed that he had discovered, in the feminine, the full accomplishment of alterity. "I think," writes Levinas, "[that] the absolutely contrary contrary [*le contraire absolument contraire*], whose contrariety is in no way affected by the relationship that can be established between it and its correlative, the contrariety that permits its terms to remain absolutely other, is the *feminine*."[12] "Alterity," he insists, "is accomplished in the feminine. The term is on the same level as, but in meaning opposed to, consciousness."[13] It is precisely for what he says here that Simone de Beauvoir, a woman and a non-Jew, takes the philosopher to task.[14]

None of the defenses of the feminine produced by Jewish men, even those adopted or extended by many Jewish women, will change much of anything in this regard. They can only make matters worse, by claiming to discern—in Nature or one or another divine plan—absolute sanction for a division of roles or distribution of images that has in fact been decreed by men and male-dominated society. Hard-working and sensible, always ready to dispense sound advice, sensitive and compassionate, modest and reserved, a guardian of the household, the "worthy wife"[15] of Proverbs, to begin with her, exists only as a function of her husband's needs. He is the one who is lucky to have found her; "she works to bring him good, not evil, all the days of her life."[16]

Man will never willingly become woman's other. He will put himself first and woman second. As wife, mother, pillar of the family and guarantor of the purity of its sexual and dietary regime, woman is bound by only a limited number of commandments. She is effectively exempt from most positive commandments, those whose observance is tied to a particular moment of the day; for instance, she does not have to recite her prayers at fixed intervals. For she must be free to do her domestic chores. It is, however, common knowledge that, in the eyes of Jewish law, the dignity of a human being is exactly proportional to the number and severity of the obligations legally incumbent upon him or her. Women do not count toward the quorum required to hold a public worship service. They are not qualified to give testimony in court proceedings. A man can take a woman to wife and then repudiate her, but a woman can never obtain a divorce unless her husband, in the last instance, consents to give her one. Women are excluded from positions of power and barred from the world of learning and study.

No doubt, rabbinical law never completely froze woman in her position in the Jewish world. To the contrary, the evolution of her status in the course of the Middle Ages testifies to a growing recognition of her needs and the necessity of protecting her against masculine caprice; it also testifies to an ambition to reduce certain flagrant inequalities. However, the fact remains that, down to the present day, the Jewish conception of the feminine, at least in its orthodox variants, has not broken with a basically essentialist, differentialist, and rather inegalitarian approach.

Woman is still the other and the other is still feminine. Woman is associated with nature and man with culture. Vis-à-vis Israel, which is masculine, the nations are feminine. Even God's androgyny does not imply any sort of symmetry or equivalence. The whole kabbalistic tradition conceives both the split in the Divine and the means of overcoming it with the help of gendered, sexual images. The task of religious man is accordingly to unify the two faces of the Divinity, male and female, thus restoring their original unity and breaking the fatal cycle of separation and exile. Yet the fact remains that the androgynous Divinity is first and foremost masculine and that any reunification of the divine also ultimately implies subordination of the feminine to the masculine principle. It is the masculine principle that is the source of all mercy and it must obviously take precedence over its opposite, the feminine principle of an extremely strict justice, which is a destructive force. In the hoped-for union of the two principles, the Feminine is sum-

moned to dissolve itself in the Masculine, to let itself
be absorbed or neutralized by it.

When the Feminine, the last of the ten emanated
divine powers, finds itself dissociated from the other
nine, it falls, irreparably, into the power of the
Demon, becoming demoniacal in its turn. Whenever
the Feminine is not subordinated to the Masculine,
which is the right side, the side of light and holiness
and the side of grace, it lurches to the left, the side of
judgment and rigor, shadows and impurity. The
people of Israel is, unmistakably, to be found on the
right: it does not lean to the left or mix with it. But
when Israel sins, the right side is humiliated and the
left breaks free. The left side, that of the Feminine, is
also that of the nations and idolatry. It is the kabbalists' "other side" . . . the side of Evil.

Conceived of as otherness, the Feminine, and
therefore Woman as well, are inevitably denigrated
and demonized. Rebellious women are demons.
Lilith, who is said to have been the first Eve, to have
been created directly from the earth, like Adam, and
to have demanded a position of complete equality
with him, has become the enemy of all women; she
threatens to strangle the new-born and tries to seduce
men in their sleep. . . . It is impossible not to detect
this twofold fear of the other and of women behind
the set of ritual regulations that shield men from all
contact with their menstruating wives. Women's idle-
ness is something to be feared, as is their idle chatter.
Women are vulnerable and impressionable, with
tastes and impulses rooted in childhood; they are eter-

nal children. Women are coquettes and temptresses as well, associated with impurity, the devil, and death.

Among the first blessings that every practicing Jewish man must recite every morning, one never fails to strike observers: "blessed art thou, our Eternal God . . . for not making me a woman." He says so exactly the way he says, "blessed art thou, our Eternal God . . . for not making me a *goy*." Masculinity is thus experienced and valorized on the same grounds as Jewishness: it is a form of election. The man's prayer accordingly means nothing more nor less than "blessed art thou, our Eternal God, for not making me other, for not making me second." The practicing Jewish woman, for her part, has to content herself with reciting the following resigned blessing: "blessed be he who has made men in accordance with his will. . . ." And, in any case, the birth of a girl can never satisfy the obligation to procreate, an obligation that Jewish law, let us add, lays on men alone, never on women. A man cannot rest assured that he has done his duty unless he has a boy or, as another school of thought has it, two boys. It is as if one had to have a son in order to be a father in the true sense. Only one's first-born son counts as one's first-born child.

Israel itself is the first-born son of the Lord, not, needless to say, his first-born daughter. In the traditional liturgy, God is the "God of our fathers," the God of Abraham, Isaac and Jacob. He is not the God of our mothers. And God himself is our Father, not our Mother. If he is the big Thou, the big interlocutor, this big Thou has a gender: he is masculine. *He* is blessed, not she. God is undeniably male because he is absolutely primary.

Yet this primacy of the Masculine comes at a paradoxical price: it is breached in its very heart, and the feminine inevitably slips through the breach to make its return. For the history of Israel and its God is a love story. It is the story of a wedding, but also of betrayal and even prostitution; it is a story of forgiveness too, and reconciliation and reunion. The Song of Songs, which would seem to celebrate the fleshly love between a man and a woman, owes its inclusion in the Biblical canon to a powerful tradition of allegorical interpretation that makes it a narrative of the spiritual love between God and his people. For God loves Israel as a man loves a woman. The Eternal himself explicitly says so, proclaiming, through the mouth of his prophets: " 'When that day comes . . . you will call me, My husband . . . I shall betroth you to Myself for ever, I shall betroth you in uprightness and justice, and faithful love and tenderness. Yes, I shall betroth you to Myself in loyalty and in the knowledge of the Eternal.' "[17] The covenant is sealed the way a marriage is. And, in this marriage, the wife's role naturally falls to Israel.

The Jewish people was not the wife of God alone; unfortunately, it was long the wife of the nations as well, this time in an eminently negative sense. The femininity of Israel, the nations' other—its "weakness," "guile," and "powers of seduction"—are also a recurrent theme in anti-Jewish discourse. Anti-

Semitism and anti-feminism have always found it easy to join hands. The contemporary aspiration to restore Jewish "virility," the emphasis put, in the pioneers' discourse and practice, on resolutely masculine or even war-like values, and Zionism's exaltation of strength and the cultivation of the soil all testify to an internalization of the anti-Semitic stereotype of the effeminate, weakly, and cowardly diasporic Jew, even as they bear witness to a fierce desire to give the lie to this stereotype once and for all. It is as if the aim were to declare to the world, in no uncertain terms: "No, the Jew is not a woman, nor does he wish to be. No, the Jew is neither a passive creature nor the blessed instrument of a God who chooses him as one chooses a bride, in order to impose his law on him; nor is he the hapless, humiliated, willing plaything of violent, iniquitous nations. No," we are told, "the Jew is a man, the master of his fate, the autonomous founder of his present and of his future as well."

This, we hardly need point out, is manifestly not the best way of liberating the Jewish male from his painful lot. But what if women were finally authorized to speak out? What if, at last, there were ears to hear them? "Hear her voice," "heed her demands,"[18] God tells Abraham one day, speaking of Abraham's wife Sarah. Was he not thereby indirectly enjoining Abraham or his descendants to undertake something like a new exile, and, in a sense, tearing him from the ancient ways once again? Has the time not finally come to invest the first injunction with a new and hitherto unsuspected meaning: "Leave your own country, your kin, and your *father's* house"?[19]

This is, at any event, the other main achievement of Jewish modernity, along with Zionism. For more than a century now, an upheaval has been underway; many of its repercussions have yet to come into view. To some, it may seem excessive, sectarian, or too typically North American. No matter. A path has now been cleared for a Jewish-feminist discourse and practice that, breaking with all essentialist constructions of femininity and refusing to reduce the feminine to the sole dimension of otherness, seeks to recast it in a primary, positive role, through either appropriation and rehabilitation, or, better yet, subversion and re-definition. The feminization of the liturgy, a reassessment of the principles and modalities of the application of Jewish law, the ordination of women as rabbis—there we have the stake of today's battles: to wrest the Jewish woman from the domain of the other, and, in the process, rethink or reinvent Judaism itself from top to bottom.

2 Exodus

Israel, Exile, and the Nations

If only you will now listen to me and keep my covenant, then out of all peoples you will become my special possession; for the whole earth is mine. You will be to me a kingdom of priests, my holy nation.

—Exodus 19: 5–6

"The Mosaic distinction," according to Jan Assmann, was the great innovation of ancient Judaism; the great innovation, in fact, of monotheism.[20] The invention of the unique, universal God abruptly reduced the other's divinities to naught. The nations became "idolaters"; their gods were not gods at all, but sheer simulacra, nothing but stone, wood, or inanimate metal. Previously, polytheism had managed to make room for everyone's divinities: anyone could recognize something like a replica of his own gods in his neighbors' and find the same higher powers concealed behind names that varied with languages and cultures. Jewish monotheism, in contrast, invented religious error. Now, suddenly, there existed a true religion and a true, unique God; by the same token, there were false religions and false gods. With this, the stage was set for a merciless struggle based on the violence of an exclusion. Facing the excluded were the chosen.

Election naturally made the scandal worse. The one God was the God of just one people. A privileged covenant had been concluded between this one God and this one people. "The Eternal is our God, the Eternal is one."[21] Was it not natural and just that Judaism should ultimately fall victim to the kind of exclusiveness it had itself promoted? That, on the stage of history, other monotheisms should in turn have appeared to affirm the oneness of the one God, while offering those excluded in the past a way to take revenge? The God of Israel had gone on to become the God of the others, the God of the nations, everyone's God—if not in actual fact, then at least potentially. Israel itself, it would be proclaimed, had lost its privilege. Christianity, the story goes, proceeded to confine it to the role of a now blind and disinherited older brother. In its turn, Islam ranged it, along with Christianity, in the camp of the flawed religions with falsified scriptures. Subject to abiding ostracism and suffering the dereliction otherwise reserved for pariahs, lepers, and the impure, Israel had to pay the heavy price of an exclusion it had itself invented. Matters are obviously not so simple. Such a one-sided representation of Jewish monotheism seriously distorts the picture. What is more, it can all too easily be made to serve as an explanation—or, worse, justification—for the most aggressive sort of theological anti-Judaism or even anti-Semitism. And it cannot make us forget that if Judaism itself cultivated an unshakable feeling of secret superiority, even in the midst of humiliation, defeat, and dispersion, it never lost sight of the universality of its message.

To begin with, while the Eternal is clearly the God of Israel, he nonetheless reigns over the whole world. The God who gives his people the Torah is also the creator of the universe. And the very Torah that lays down the terms of the Covenant is also a narrative of beginnings—the beginnings of humanity. The covenant concluded with Israel on Mount Sinai does not invalidate the one concluded with Noah, the new Adam and the father of all men, which stipulates that God will never again unloose a cataclysm as destructive as the Flood. The covenant of Mount Sinai extends and fulfills this first covenant; it by no means abrogates it. Quite the contrary: in this business, everyone has his place and a role to play. Like Israel, men, all men, are bound to God by a covenant. And this covenant requires that every man respect a law. The law in question, says the tradition, consists of seven commandments known as the commandments of "Noah's sons": the obligation to establish a legal system; the prohibition of blasphemy, idolatry, murder, theft, and incest and adultery; and a prohibition against eating any member torn from a living animal.

The great medieval jurist Moses Maimonides holds that the non-Jew who respects the terms of the covenant concluded with Noah, fulfilling these seven minimal obligations, may be considered one of the righteous and wise among the nations and will benefit from salvation—on condition, to be sure, that he acts in the awareness that these commandments are of divine origin and were revealed to Moses! It should be added that the application of Noachide law is a much more demanding matter, perhaps, than appears at first sight. Does it not presuppose monotheism, and a monotheism that is perhaps stricter than Christianity's, with the three persons of its Trinity and its taste for representation? Yet the fact remains that the commandments known as the commandments of "Noah's sons," which are not understood simply as an expression of natural law, confer authentic legal and religious status on the non-Jewish other in Jewish law, without requiring that he convert to Judaism. There is no need to become a Jew in order to be saved. It is enough to be, fully, a human being.

Similarly, rabbinical Judaism would never teach that election was an absolutely non-transferable privilege. The non-Jew who wishes to join the community of Israel may do so. No-one will seek him out; his task will even be made more complicated than it is; if need be, the obstacles on his path will be multiplied. Yet, if his intentions reveal themselves to be pure and disinterested, the door will be opened for him; place will be made for the other, who will be transformed into the same. A certain strand in the Jewish tradition, which privileges physical descent and *jus sanguinis,* will perhaps hesitate to acknowledge the convert's full equality with the natural-born Jew. Thus for Judah Halevi, the fideist, the Judaism of a non-Jew who has become a Jew is merely the best to be had in the way of imitations of Judaism. The convert will, to be sure, "approach God very closely" and has a fair claim to being "one of God's intimates,"[22] but he will never be capable of prophecy, which, for Halevi, is the very heart of Jewishness. Yet, on these questions, Halevi and his co-thinkers represent only one of the voices of Judaism. There is another, for which the non-Jew who becomes a Jew was, at bottom, merely a hidden Jew who did not know himself for what he was: a potential Jew. And even if none of his ancestors was present at the theophany of Mount Sinai, his *constellation* was. The convert who, like any other Jew, is a disciple of Moses, may be fully integrated into the genealogy of Israel. His Jewish descendants will plead in his favor. And he will easily find his place in what constitutes, according to a different tradition of the definition of Jewish identity, the backbone of Judaism: not prophecy, but the transmission of rabbinical knowledge. For to become a "doctor" of the Law is clearly the highest distinction to which one can aspire in the Jewish world. Were not some of the greatest masters of the oral Law, some of those who most powerfully shaped it, descended of proselytes themselves—such as, at least on certain accounts, Rabbi Meir or Rabbi Akiva?

The choice, however, is not between these two alternatives, which are too starkly distinguished: on the one hand, to assume one's identity as a human being, a simple descendant of Noah, in the absence of all reference to any positive religion whatever, or, on the other, to assume one's identity as a Jew, a descendant of Abraham and a follower of the revealed, transmitted doctrine. For Judaism stands in an ambiguous relation to the two monotheisms that claim to have replaced it. Neither pure Noachidism nor authentic Judaism, Christianity and Islam, as theologies of the entre-deux, are not condemned without appeal. Curiously, a certain place is reserved for them too, at least provisionally. The reason is that they are both other and very similar.

The Jews of the Middle Ages undeniably knew this odd feeling of proximity and intimate relation. They often gave expression to it, angrily or sardonically. The famous medieval anti-Gospels of the Jews, better known as the *Toledot Yeshu*, bear witness, above all, to this exasperated, irate acknowledgement of resemblance. Violent, insulting, brutal, and baroque, these parodies of the life of Jesus, which rehabilitate Judas, seem to be inspired by pure, unrelieved hatred for Christians. The Jesus they present—a child of impurity, the son of a sexually abused mother—is described as a "bastard." Moreover, the tragedy of his conception becomes the tragedy of his life. If, by his mother, he is plainly a child of Israel, he remains fatherless for all time. Jesus is a genealogical invalid whose infirmity prevents him from finding a legitimate place among his people. Hence he takes refuge in blasphemy and, through his own actions, condemns himself to death. A fatherless child, Jesus invents a heavenly Father for himself. A bastard, he gives birth to a spiritual bastard, Christianity—which is and is not Israel.

This is the essential point (if we ignore the anger). In most of the narratives that have come down to us, the members of the nascent Nazarene community are consistently presented as children of Israel. Only rarely do these stories mention the conversion of Gentiles to the new faith. It is as if the stakes of the struggle, at least at the outset, were first and foremost internal. The objective of the Jews who, beginning with Judas, remain faithful to their religion is precisely to consummate a rupture and make it irreversible, so that it will no longer be possible to be both a Jew and a Christian. Those who initiate the rupture are not, in these narratives, Jews who have rallied to Jesus, but Jews who have remained faithful to the Torah. And it is a faithful Jew, Simon Peter, who sacrifices himself for the good cause. A sort of Marrano *avant la lettre,* an authentic Jew (not Jesus, the bastard Jew) pretends to be an emissary of Jesus in order to endow the Church with a practice and a theology which, though doubtless quite rudimentary, suffice to draw a line for once and all between the Church, a multitude "as countless as the sands of the seashore,"[23] and the little that remains of faithful Israel.

Who could fail to observe that the propagation of these religions, whatever the original intentions involved, promoted the eradication—partial and incomplete, to be sure, yet real enough—of idolatry and polytheism?

Here is Halevi's account:

> God has a secret and wise design concerning us, which should be compared to the wisdom hidden in the seed which falls into the ground, where it undergoes an external transformation into earth, water and dirt, without leaving a trace for him who looks down upon it. It is, however, the seed itself which transforms earth and water into its own substance, carries it from one stage to another, until it refines the elements and transforms them into something like itself, casting off husks, leaves, etc. and allowing the pure core to appear, capable of bearing the Divine Influence. The original seed produced the tree bearing fruit resembling that from which it had been produced. In the same manner, the law of Moses transforms each one who honestly follows it, though it may externally repel him. The nations merely serve to introduce and pave the way for the expected Messiah, who is the fruition, and they will all become his fruit. Then, if they acknowledge him, they will become one tree.[26]

Maimonides, for his part, affirms rather that:

> It is beyond the human mind to fathom the designs of the Creator. . . . All these matters relating to Jesus of Nazareth and the Ishmaelite who came after him only served to clear the way for King

Messiah, to prepare the whole world to worship God with one accord. . . . Thus the Messianic hope, the Torah, and the commandments have become familiar topics—topics of conversation [among the inhabitants] of the far isles and many peoples, uncircumcised of heart and flesh. They are discussing these matters and the commandments of the Torah. Some say, "those commandments were true, but have lost their validity and are no longer binding." Others declare that they had an esoteric meaning and were not intended to be taken literally; that the Messiah has already come and revealed their occult significance. But when the true King Messiah appears . . . they will forthwith recant and realize that they have inherited naught but lies from their fathers, that their prophets and forebears led them astray.[27]

In Halevi, the truth lies buried in Christianity and Islam in the form of a seed. This seed will sprout, flower, and at last reveal itself, a fruit stripped of its skin, for what it is: Jewish. This is possible thanks only to the dispersion of Israel everywhere, for Israel is the seed disseminated among the nations; through its mediation, the nations are transformed into Israel. In Maimonides, Christianity and Islam consist of errors and lies which, despite themselves, are compounded with truth, and, unexpectedly, these errors and lies prepare the advent of the truth. In any case, both Halevi and Maimonides assign Christianity and Islam genuine value as forms of "messianic preparation." Thus Christians and Moslems are co-opted. They are en route toward the same—toward the abolition of the "Mosaic distinction," the resolution of all difference, otherness, and conflict, in the at last universal worship of the one God.

> I have resolved to bring you up out of the misery of Egypt into the country of the Canaanites . . . a land flowing with milk and honey.
> —Exodus 3:17

In the nineteenth century, broad, profoundly secularized segments of the Jewish world, more impatient than the others, refused to content themselves with the glorious but abstract prospect of deliverance and final reconciliation held out by traditional Jewish thought: Israel as priest among the nations, establishing itself in exile in order to accomplish, slowly and almost secretly, its work of redemption. . . . Could this ideal reconciliation of the particular and the universal not be realized in some more immediate fashion? Should other, more concrete means not be sought for reconciling self-affirmation with openness to the other? Was it not time simply to jettison the old models? Had the wait not already lasted too long?

The French variant of emancipated Judaism chose to regard the French Revolution and the proclamation of its grand principles as the first step toward a secular republican realization of the messianic ideals of eternal Judaism. In Central and Eastern Europe, where, for too long, emancipation was beyond reach, many young Jews joined the ranks of the socialist and revolutionary movements. Here they were a pioneering presence, a source of ferment, and a catalyst.

Would the Jewish problem not be automatically resolved with the concrete realization, here below, of social justice—with the emancipation of the whole human race?

Zionism summoned its adherents to make a more radical change of direction. With its advent, Judaism strove to disappear as a theological and historical exception so that it might be reborn as a simple demand for nationhood. The Jewish people was summoned to become fully itself while at last establishing balanced relations with the rest of the world; it was to do so, in Zionist perspective, by achieving normalcy, that is, by coming to resemble all the other nations, with a territory and state. The builders of the nation set out to forge a new Jew, a Jew who, after returning to his own country, would no longer feel the least nostalgia for the experience of exile or the least attachment to the land of his birth. This new Jew was summoned to become an Israeli. Refusing to shoulder the weight of an imaginary responsibility for the world, he would first take his own destiny in hand.

It is easy to guess the price of this metamorphosis: it implied the negation of diasporic otherness. The Israeli would be a product of Israel alone. He would be born of a project, not a history thousands of years old that had unfolded far from the cradle of the nation, in lands in which the exiled Jews invented surrogate Jerusalems to compensate for the forgetting of the divine promise and the original holy Jerusalem to which so few ever found their way. Who did not have his Jerusalem? From Vilnius to Sarajevo, from Tétuan to

Amsterdam, countless cities found themselves invested with a diasporic holiness. Once they had returned to the land that they had never laid eyes on but had always remembered, the Jews could simply wipe out this past and start over. The melting pot was the nation, a unified nation without diasporic roots. The Zionist dream did not hesitate to impugn the Diaspora and its history and to thrust them into the shadows. Just one language and just one country. But how were the Jews to be shorn of their diasporic otherness? This proved to be an impossible task, and yet a necessary one for Zionist ideologues, who saw no other way of forging the new man they fervently wished to bring into being. Do all ideologies not seek to replace the Creator, even if this means that they must become secular creators in their turn? At all costs, this new man had to be created to replace the old one and blot out his very memory: such, in this instance, were man's inordinate ambitions for man. It was as if the vestiges of the old man thwarted realization of the new plans. The twentieth century paid a heavy price, in many different parts of the world, for inventing a new man who never really was new. That is why Zionism rewrites history, ringing changes on the myth of a continuous Jewish presence in the land of Israel: a land supposedly inhabited from the beginning of time by a people that was in fact long absent from it. This absence had to be forgotten, the better to establish a presence.

The better to love this land, which had long been a mere memory, the new Jew was supposed to identify with it physically. The *sabra,* the native, was supposed to become one with its landscapes, fauna, flora, smells, and history. The result was to be a seamless fusion, total osmosis, capable of invigorating Zionism and the soil of the new nation. Myths came to the rescue of this ideal, which was assigned to a diasporic people that, over the centuries, had lost its feel for the land, a land supposed to belong rightfully to a nation and state of the Jews. In this race to secure a new identity, the Jew was effaced in favor of the vigorous, athletic, healthy, valiant Israeli. The Jew, the other who had not become part of the new, victorious nation, was described in terms that, to some extent, recalled anti-Semitic stereotypes. The Jew of exile bore within himself traces of the ghetto, of a life that was a far cry from the conquerors' ideal, and of a fragility inherited from his long wanderings far from his ancestral soil. Puny, sickly, and passive, he was, in sum, the antithesis of his reconstructed counterpart, who had been born in different climes. All these clichés served to distance him from the one who would, from now on, rank as the true Jew, the Jew in the full, legitimate sense of the word—who was in fact just the new Israeli. Even those who had been persecuted for being Jews in the dark years of the war had, in the early period, no claim to compassion upon their arrival in Israel. They embodied an abhorred past which the new Jew owed it to himself to cover up. Yet, willy nilly, the immigrant always came dragging his diasporic past behind him; his descendants, born in the new land, inherited something of it, even if only vaguely. Once the force of Zionism was spent, this past came rushing back.

The tie with the experience of exile was, obviously, never really severed; it was continually reinforced by immigration. Israel was unable to break with either its past or the Diaspora, the mother who had nursed it. Even if they have become strangers to each other, diasporic Jews and Israelis have a shared history, which, albeit remote, is still present. The Israelis were once again to identify with their own Jewishness, down to the very appropriation of the experience of the Holocaust, which they had rejected for a moment—a brief one, to be sure—in hopes of attaining the Israeliness that the founding fathers had so desired. Hence the memory of the Diaspora inevitably became a part of the identity of the Israeli, who later set out for places far from Israel in quest of his family history. This horizon, this distant elsewhere, has been drawing steadily closer. Without the Diaspora, there can be no Jewishness—and no Israeliness, either. In the crazed hope of resuming a repressed trajectory, the native-born Israeli crosses oceans and traipses through exotic lands the better to live out his Israeli identity—as if someone had stolen a part of himself. He strikes out to discover his other, often in places where Jews are no longer to be found today, so that he may at last live in harmony with this land which is never really his and which eludes him, even if he also needs it.

Today, the Jew of exile is less foreign than he once was for the Israeli, who is in the process of re-discovering that other part of himself constituted by his Jewishness. For many diasporic Jews, the Israeli is a superior "double" who is envied, mythologized, and glorified. He is an other who, from afar, stands guard over their illusory security. He is an other self who often seems foreign, yet is regarded with a benevolent eye. Israel is a part of Jewish identity in the Diaspora. It is an element constitutive of the new plurality of loyalties that is so common among our contemporaries. Few diasporic Jews are prepared to go live in Israel, but many maintain a passionate re-lationship with this other at once close and remote, strange and familiar, to which they feel bound, even when they are not practicing Jews, by the slender threads of Judaism and religion rather than by a shared history on a common soil. As for Israelis, many today express their sense of closeness to the Diaspora by trying to share the experiences their families once had, either in the religious domain or outside it. Both Israelis and diasporic Jews rewrite their histories and reformulate their identities, but out of step with each other. The diasporic Jews in-vent an imaginary Israeliness. The Israelis transcend this invented Israeliness in order to rediscover the Jewishness of which they were long deprived by a Zionist ideology and practice whose goal was funda-mentally secular—even if, in order to attract Jews to Palestine and, later, to Israel, the Zionists had to tap

the old stock of hope that had for centuries nour-
ished a people in exile. Unsure of themselves, Israeliness and Jewishness are trying to find each other in
this exchange of regards.

Has Israel therefore become a nation like the others? Does it unflinchingly assume all the limits that its
new situation poses and all the duties that it imposes?
Have the days of hesitation and ambivalence truly
come to an end? There is good reason to doubt it. It is
as if the ambiguity that, yesterday, colored the relationship of the Jewish people to the nations had today
insensibly yielded to a new and, in some sense, internal ambiguity: one that marks the Jewish people's relationship to itself, the mirror alterities of Israeli and
Jew, the state of Israel and the Diaspora.

The nations, however, can never be forgotten.
They are there, right there, present in the familiar-
and-yet-alien figure of the other inhabitant of the
same land: the Palestinian. They are also there in the
guise of the regional or international powers that observe the wrenching conflicts of this infernal couple
and claim, in one way or another, the right to play a
role in shaping its future. What place is to be reserved
for the other, the foreigner, the resident alien? Em-
phatically, the question has not lost its urgency.
Where is the answer to be sought? In the brutal affirmation of a newly acquired strength or in a meditation on the long centuries of an exile with which, try
as one might, it has not really proven possible to
break?

You shall not wrong or oppress an alien, for you were once aliens yourselves in the land of Egypt.

—Exodus 22:20

How precious is the memory of exile! For it is not just a memory of humiliation and suffering. It cannot simply serve to justify and sustain a legitimate concern for self, a desire for a territory and a refuge. Was the other's law always so cruel and unjust for the Jews? And what does its very injustice, demonstrated all too often, have to teach us? What course of action is dictated by the searing memory of our own trials or those of our ancestors? Withdrawal into ourselves? The arrogance of an autonomy without limits?

To be honest, quite the opposite, if we are to believe the Bible, which takes, precisely, the memory of the exile and the sojourn in Egypt as the basis for one whole segment of its ethics—indeed, for the whole of its ethics. It is because the other treated you as an enemy, slave, or traitor when you dwelt in his country and under his rule, and because you remember it (for it is your duty to remember it), that you will not treat the foreigner living in your midst as an enemy, slave, or traitor once you have become rulers in your turn. Those whose lot it was to suffer the burden of discriminatory laws cannot inflict similar laws on those who happen to come under their sway: "As for the assembly, there shall be for both you and the resident alien a single statute, a perpetual statute throughout your generations; you and the alien shall be alike before the Eternal. You and the alien who resides with you shall have the same law and the same ordinance."[28]

If the Hebrew and the foreigner are equals before the Eternal in the land of Canaan, the reason is that the Hebrew remains a foreigner in the Eternal's eyes, even in the place that has been allotted to him, even on the land in which his presence is at last fully legitimate: "no land shall be sold in perpetuity, for the land is mine; with me you are but aliens and tenants."[29] From this standpoint, there is no escaping exile, not even in the land of Israel. In God's eyes, the exile's condition is forever inseparable from the Jewish condition. Indeed, it is inseparable from the human condition as such. Does human history, as the Bible delights in telling us, not begin with an exile, the expulsion of our first ancestors from the Garden of Eden? Similarly, will the end of the Jews' exile, should it ever end, not be, by the same token, the end of everybody's? The final gathering up in the days of Redemption will not only bring together the scattered sons of Israel. "I will gather others to them," the Eternal declares, "besides those already gathered."[30] "The sons of the foreigners," or, at any rate, "those who join themselves to the Eternal" and love and serve him, will be brought to his holy mountain as well, for his house "shall be called a house of prayer for all peoples."[31]

Yet it is not only from the somber face of exile or the painful experience of subjection, oppression, and persecution that the Bible draws the lesson of compassion for the foreigners whom the Hebrews came to shelter in their turn, granting them a right to special protection because of their vulnerability. The experience of exile had a bright side as well. It too was, in certain circumstances, a positive experience of hospitality. In making room for banished, dispersed Israel, the nations sometimes displayed indulgence and generosity. There was a reason for the fact that, while wandering in the wilderness, the Hebrews were suddenly overcome by homesickness for the country that they had just fled; a reason for the fact that, although now nurtured on manna and freedom, they looked back with regret on the fish, cucumbers, melons, leeks, onions, and garlic that they used to eat in the land of those who had reduced them to slavery. . . . Egypt itself was, at least for a time, a hospitable, promising land. This too is something that the Hebrews are enjoined to remember: "you shall not abhor any of the Egyptians, for you were an alien residing in their land."[32] The memory of servitude must not obliterate that of the generous welcome the Hebrews received when Pharaoh opened the gates of his country to them after their flight from the land of Canaan, ravaged by drought and famine. The foreign ruler is not to be reduced to the unequivocal image of the persecutor, even if that is what he finally became. In the memory of the Jews who were forced to flee or in that of their descendants, all the countries in which Jews were oppressed continue to wear the halo of a Golden Age that is never entirely imaginary. This holds for the Morocco of the Moroccan Jew in exile and the Hungary of the Hungarian Jew in exile. It holds even for Germany, despite the bottomless pit of horror into which, as everyone knows, it cast European Jewry, and despite the incurable wound it inflicted on the Jewish people. In the contemporary Jewish imagination, Germany is still decked out in the shining colors of a "symbiosis" which, rightly or wrongly, continues to serve as a model.

Moreover, the Biblical laws do not just consist of warnings; they do not just prohibit hating, wronging, or oppressing foreigners. They include a genuinely positive commandment to love foreigners. It is true that, as formulated in Leviticus, this commandment would seem to apply only to immigrants, to foreigners who are socially vulnerable because they have left their own country and taken up residence among the Hebrews organized in an autonomous state.[33] In post-Biblical interpretations, however, the injunction to love foreigners holds in the opposite situation as well; it is also a duty for the weak in their relations with the strong. It extends to all foreigners, including members of the all-powerful non-Jewish societies in which the rigors of exile forced dispersed Israel to reside. Thus the rabbis never ceased to teach the faithful respect and humanity in their daily relations with the non-Jews in whose midst they had settled. "We must support the poor of the heathen and visit their sick," the Babylonian Talmud clearly says, "for the sake of keeping the peace."[34]

What we see here is by no means just prudence or apprehensive civility toward non-Jews perceived as potential threats. There is also an affirmation of the primacy of the ideal of peace, the only authentic peace being that which one builds with the other and which it is incumbent on the weak as much as the powerful to help establish, notwithstanding the differences in their status and strength. Similarly, the concern that the Jews have always shown for the stability and prosperity of their host countries, expressed in very official fashion in the synagogal liturgical prayer beseeching God to bless the state and its current leaders, should not be interpreted as a patriotism dictated by circumstance or selfish motives. It is rooted in the recommendations that the prophet Jeremiah gave the exiles from Judah who settled in Babylon: "Build houses and live in them; plant gardens and eat what they produce. Take wives and have sons and daughters. . . . seek the welfare of the city where I have sent you into exile, and pray to the Lord on its behalf, for in its peace you will find your peace."[35]

Exile required the Jews to define happiness for themselves and to formulate their own demand for justice in the framework of interdependencies involving both Jews and non-Jews, the community of the dispersed of Israel and the surrounding national or state entities which sheltered them. In an even broader sense, going beyond these perhaps still too local allegiances, it was in fact the human, the whole of humanity, and, beyond humanity, the whole of creation, which were the objects of the Jewish aspiration to *shalom*, true integrity and peace: an integrity and a peace that, as the Prophets announce, will make swords into plow-shares and bring the wolf and the lamb to graze peacefully side by side.

Yet this universalism is only one side of a coin that plainly has two. However pronounced and authentic the ethical demand and the hope for unlimited harmony, they do not banish fear of non-Jews; non-Jews are still perceived as a threat, down to the seductive fascination that they inevitably exert, in certain historical contexts, on the most refined minds in the Jewish community and sometimes even on a majority of its members. Hence another exegetical strand, as fully attested as the one just mentioned, invites us to restrict the field of application of texts which, at first sight, seem so favorable to "foreigners." Is it, in fact, the foreigner in the broadest sense that the lovely verse of Exodus at the beginning of this section enjoins the Hebrews not to wrong or oppress? As in many other Biblical passages, the word employed here authorizes any number of interpretive reversals. *Ger,* a term designating the resident alien, is a word that post-Biblical Hebrew invested with a meaning which, precisely, neutralizes its "foreignness." In rabbinical Hebrew, *ger* is used not for the foreigner per se, but rather for the convert to Judaism, the proselyte: it means, in other words, the foreigner who no longer is one, the naturalized foreigner. Hence it would be easy to displace all the compassion and generosity called for by the Scriptural injunctions from the person of the foreigner to that of the non-Jew who has become a Jew, the metaphorical immigrant who has cut the ties that bound him to the community of his birth and taken his place alongside Israel beneath the wings of the divine Presence. It would thus be the proselyte who should be, not wronged or oppressed, but loved: he should not be reminded of his origins and his feelings should be spared as much as possible, either because he is known to be more vulnerable and sensitive than others, or, on the contrary, for fear that offending him will make him relapse into the scandalous practices that he has just abandoned.

Yet this *ger* is a curious figure. He is eminently ambiguous. By making him the privileged or even exclusive beneficiary of the love due the foreigner, rabbinical Judaism would seem to close itself to the outside and withdraw into itself. At the same time, however, quite the opposite is true. As a naturalized foreigner, the *ger* is a Jew who remains a foreigner. He is acknowledged to be a Jew and is protected because he is a foreigner. In Hebrew, the way to say "to become a Jew" is "to become a *ger*." It is as if, by an odd paradox, the best way of becoming a Jew, for a foreigner, is to become a foreigner, a *ger*. This is how a foreigner becomes truly Jewish. For to be Jewish is, at the deepest level, to be "foreign." This fundamental ambiguity of being-Jewish is revealed by the seemingly unfinished trajectory of the proselyte. Can natural-born Jews not criticize him for having worshiped Baal and Nebo only yesterday and speaking of the Torah today, when there is still "pig-meat sticking out from between his teeth?"[36] But would he not find it easy, precisely, to reply to his adversary: "Have you forgotten that you too were once an alien in the land of Egypt? That the forefathers of your ancestor Abraham were all idolaters themselves? Are you not criticizing me for a weakness that affects you, the natural-born Jew, as much as it does me?"

Thus, thanks to a *mise-en-abyme* and a complicated play of mirrors, the figure of the Jew and that of the "foreigner" seem, curiously, to coincide. Whenever Judaism closes itself off, it opens itself up still further. Whenever it seems to turn its face from the foreigner, it is in fact busy welcoming him—better, recognizing him within itself. The image of the *ger*, the "resident alien," amounts to a reminder of a basic truth, one that reappears at the very moment that it seems to have been swept aside: to be Jewish is to recall the presence of the foreigner in oneself and to grant him the right to dwell in oneself. The border is fixed and seems closed; in fact, it is open. It is as if it did not run between the Jew and the "foreigner," but rather cut through the Jew himself.

The history of the Jews testifies again and again to this permeability. And if rabbinical law and historical circumstance have hardly favored individual conversions, the development of Jewish civilization over the centuries bears witness to the broad scope of much more spectacular phenomena of cultural naturalization and assimilation of the other. For, in the Jewish world, the love of the "foreigner" has made itself felt as, above all, a love of foreign lands, the temptation of co-optation, and the partial or total adoption of the values and aspirations of the alien society of which the Jews were ultimately an integral part, even if they were "different" and subjugated. Far from living cut off from their milieu, and even when, as sometimes happened, they were socially excluded from it, the Jews often loved what it loved: in many cases, their own cultural accomplishments can be explained only if they are seen in this wider context. Is there anything more "Jewish" than the poetry of a Moses Ibn Ezra, the theology of a Judah Halevi, the legal studies of a Moses Maimonides? But should we therefore forget that Ibn Ezra was doubtless the most Arabophile of the poets of the Spanish Jews' Golden Age, that Halevi was steeped in the very philosophical conceptions whose limitations he delighted in pointing out, or that the methodical approach of the jurist Maimonides certainly owes a great deal to the Greco-Arab thought that he had been raised on? Is there a single period in Jewish history when the Jews did not embrace, in one way or another, openly or covertly, the achievements of an essentially "foreign" wisdom?

The Iberian episode of medieval Judaism does not provide the sole illustration of this astonishing openness, this genuine "love of the foreigner," but it does provide a superb illustration of it. And the denunciations, by the staunchest traditionalists, of the aberrations this "love" is supposed to have bred—the stigmatization of philosophy as an impious, or, at any rate, dangerous science, and of Averroism as a school of doubt and relativism—changes nothing here. What is more "Spanish" than Spanish Judaism? What, in a later period, was more "Italian" than Italian Judaism, more "French" than French Judaism, more "German" than German Judaism? Of course, there is always some means of neutralizing the "foreignness" of what has been borrowed. Thus medieval Judaism was to invent the myth of the lost science; it takes it for granted that any true science or authentic philosophy must have its origins in Abraham and his descendants. Aristotle was, in fact, a disciple of Moses. Were the medieval Jews pale imitators of the Arabs and Greeks? Not at all! The riches that had been temporarily lost by Israel and passed on to the nations had simply been restored to their first, legitimate owners in the framework of a re-appropriation rather than an appropriation. Later, in the contemporary period, French Judaism would ultimately adopt a rather similar strategy, affirming that it recognized, in the French Republic, the realization of the ancient hopes nurtured for centuries and finally transmitted to the Gentiles by the people of Israel. . . .

What strange malleability, what astonishing permeability characterizes the Jewish world that exile inextricably intertwined with the nations! Yet, at the same time, its cosmology and theology, sacred history and religious practice bear the marks of an obsessive demand for separation . . .

3 Leviticus

The Ideal of Separation and the Ethical Demand

. . . the purpose of the law being to make a distinction between the unclean and the clean, between living creatures that may be eaten and those that may not be eaten.

—Leviticus 11:47

If the world was ever in fact created, it may very well have been created ex nihilo. There is really no a priori reason for denying a God supposed to be almighty the power to accomplish such a prodigious feat. Yet the fact is that a reading of the Genesis narrative as a meditation on the great organizing principles of the Law given to Israel and recorded, notably, in Leviticus brings out the figure of a God who "makes distinctions" much more than that of a Creator God.

God divides the light from the darkness, separates the waters that are above from those that are below, and brings forth the dry land by confining the sea within limits. The lights that he sets in the space of the firmament serve to distinguish day from night and the seasons from one another, as well as to keep the count of the years. Every living species, vegetable or animal, reproduces itself in its seed, distinct from the others. Man is taken from the dust of the earth. The creation of woman herself is, first of all, an act of separation: she is a "rib" or "side" of man that has been taken from him. And this whole labor of creation, which is very good in God's own eyes, culminates in the distinction of secular and sacred time, the six weekdays and the *shabat*.

It is not only in the history of the world that distinction is at work. It is active in the history of men as well. Since Noah, and, even more plainly, since the episode of the Tower of Babel, human history has been the history of a diversification and individualization of the nations, now dispersed "over the face of all the earth," each speaking its own tongue and incapable of understanding those of the others.[37] This process is doubtless an evil or, at any rate, punishment for an evil—punishment for the will to power that drove men to unite in the face of God and against God in hopes of reaching the top of the heavens. But the story does not end there: distinction may yet bring salvation. For God distinguishes the distinguished. He tears Abraham out of the land of his birth. He distinguishes Isaac from his brother Ishmael, and, later,

Jacob from his brother Esau. He leads Israel out of Egypt and distinguishes it by giving it the Law. And the Law too is, for the people that God has chosen for himself, an imperative to distinguish. It enjoins Israel to bless him Who separates and to engage, every day, in a practice of distinction as a form of human participation in the process of Creation, a form of reparation and redemption. It enjoins it to continue to distinguish what must be distinguished and to replace chaos with order on the way leading to true unity and a horizon of harmony.

The confusion of distinct kinds is the greatest imaginable evil, because it represents a return to chaos. Everything has its place, all borders must be respected. There is no blurring the line between the same and the other. The rejection of the hybrid and the mixed is omnipresent. It is forbidden to wear cloth in which flax, of vegetable origin, is blended with wool, of animal origin. It is forbidden to sow different kinds of seeds in the same field. It is forbidden to make different kinds of animals breed. It is forbidden to yoke an ox and a donkey together to plow the fields. Similarly, a woman must not wear men's apparel, nor a man put on women's clothes, "for whoever does such things is abhorrent to the Eternal, your God."[38] This prohibition has multiple consequences. A man must refrain from plucking out even a single gray hair, because that is what women do to make themselves beautiful. Are feminization of the masculine and masculinization of the feminine so many ways of blurring a distinction posed as original and absolute? Perhaps. But matters are certainly more complicated, inasmuch as all ornament and finery treated as "feminine" by local custom are, according to the Law, forbidden for men, and vice versa. It is the principle of distinction that reigns absolute. The ways in which it is applied, in contrast, can vary ad infinitum. A man may look at his reflection in the mirror if local custom has it that men, and not just women, look at their reflections in the mirror. If this practice is culturally marked as typically feminine, he may not.

Every individual must play the masculine or feminine role that has fallen to his or her lot. It is the inversion or introversion of roles that introduces chaos. It seems safe to assume that this is what is hidden beneath the prohibition of (masculine) homosexuality: "if a man lies with a male as with a woman, both of them have committed an abomination; they shall be put to death; their blood is upon them."[39] The crime here consists in treating a man as if he were a woman, or, if one is a man, in agreeing to take the woman's role. It is a crime, as well, to use an animal as if it were a human being. Men are forbidden to bestow their sperm on animals; women are forbidden to couple with them. The laws against adultery and prostitution both rule out mixture and confusion and bear witness to a haunting fear of the loss of distinction. One man's wife cannot simultaneously be another's; one woman cannot be the wife of all men. There is, finally, the prohibition of incest and the rule of endogamy. They seem to pull in opposite directions. Both, however, aim to preserve distinction. To refrain from committing incest maintains differences in status, safeguards the social order, and ensures its reproduction and permanence by preserving it from chaos: "therefore a man leaves his father and his mother and clings to his wife, and they become one flesh."[40] To marry within the group, especially if this group is, like the Jewish people, a dispersed minority, guarantees its survival, protecting its identity from admixture and dissolution.

The faithful Jew's whole life is marked by this demand for distinction. Israel will be able fully to realize its mission among the nations, if it has one, only if it remains separate from them. Moreover, many hold that this mission itself consists in the attempt to separate the sacred from the profane, to rescue the sparks of the divine that have fallen into the here below from their baleful union with darkness and Evil. Only by separating the sacred from the profane can one extend the realm of the sacred and reduce the profane to what it is: non-being. For many, every gesture of daily life should become a vehicle for this labor of separation and sacralization. This is clearly the purpose of the extraordinary exactness and the all-inclusive character of the many different stipulations of the Law: their aim is to allow the Jew to distinguish the clean from the unclean or to cleanse what has been sullied (as a result, precisely, of a mingling of the clean and the unclean), to distinguish the sacred from the profane and sanctify the profane. The most "animalistic" functions of our bodies cannot be humanized unless they are put in the service of the Divine, that is, of distinction.

This might well be the meaning, or one of the meanings, of a system teeming with rules that usually astound the layman, when they do not shock him: the whole set of extremely rigorous dietary laws known as *kashrut*. *Kashrut* has its roots in the Bible, but rabbinical tradition has made it extraordinarily richer and more complicated. Here again, it is a question of distinguishing the clean from the unclean. But what is the unclean? It is, first and foremost, blood. Blood is life; it is therefore sacred. However, the effusion of blood from a body that it has previously animated causes death or signifies that what might have been a birth has not taken place; in these instances, blood becomes unclean. Such is the blood of a murdered man, which "cries" out for vengeance from the ground "which has opened its mouth to receive" it.[41] Such is the blood of a woman who has not been fecundated; dissociated from the work of life, her blood leaves her during menstruation and puts her in a state of ritual uncleanliness. Such is the blood of the slaughtered animal, which it is absolutely forbidden to eat. "For the life of every creature is the blood which is in its body; therefore I have said to the people of Israel: You shall not eat the blood of any creature."[42] Ritualizing slaughter, entrusting it to those who have the religious authorization to carry it out, slitting animals' throats so as to drain them of the last drop of their blood, salting and carefully washing every part of a slaughtered animal which is to be eaten, all this serves only one end: that of transforming the carcass into meat and legitimizing an act which could otherwise only be described as murder. For the vegetarian ideal haunts Biblical and rabbinical culture. Authorizing Noah and his descendants to eat the flesh of animals was just a concession to the violence of humankind: in the messianic age, the wolf and the lamb will graze together and even the lion will live on the grass of the fields.

Jews are therefore careful not to eat the bloody meat that the Gentiles eat. To do so would be to let the separate domains of life and death encroach on each other more than they should; it would be to attack not only life, but the principle informing it. This imperative of restriction and separation is also at work in all the practices that rabbinical law derives from the Biblical command "you shall not boil a kid in its mother's milk."[43] For any mixture of milk and meat is forbidden. Milk and meat cannot be used as ingredients in the same dish, eaten in the course of the same meal, or even prepared or served on the same plate. Every practicing family therefore has two rigorously distinct sets of kitchen utensils. After eating a meat dish, no orthodox Jew eats dairy food for a fixed period that, in certain traditions, can run as long as six hours. Orthodox Jews are therefore forbidden to eat a large number of dishes of the kind that abound in, for example, French cuisine. Thus they are forbidden to eat at the table of the Gentiles. For, here too, what is at issue is of course separation from the Gentiles and, at the same time, a distinction between the spheres of death (meat, spilled blood) and life (milk, which is also blood; yet milk, when it flows from the body, does not cause death, but, quite the contrary, bestows life).

That said, Biblical and rabbinical dietary law is infinitely richer and more complex, so that it is not always easy to make out its coherence or the principle governing it. As a rule, this system is put in the category of inexplicable imperatives that must be obeyed for no other reason than that God has uttered them. Medieval and modern Judaism have nevertheless tried, more or less successfully, to grasp the logic of these rules on spiritual and ethical grounds or even in terms of hygiene. Most such attempts leave the reader unsatisfied. The Bible provides a list of the kinds of poultry that must not be eaten. It is not easy to discern its logic. Similarly, why, among the four-footed animals, may one eat only the herbivorous ruminants with horned hooves that are completely cloven? This rule excludes, among other animals, the star of the menu of the whole Christian West, the pig: for, although pigs have cloven hooves, they are not ruminants. Why, among the creatures that dwell in the water, can one eat only those with fins and scales, a rule that excludes shellfish, mollusks, etc.? Is it that the prohibited foods are unhealthy? Or is what is involved simply asceticism, a way of teaching the Jews to master their instincts? Do these unclean animals embody evil passions, such as an inclination to commit murder or the cruelty characteristic of birds of prey and carnivorous four-footed animals, passions we would run the risk of strengthening in ourselves in coming to resemble what we eat? Or is it rather, as modern anthropology suggests, that this division between the clean and the unclean stems from a systematic representation of the world authorizing the consumption of only those living creatures supposed to be best adapted to their environment, especially as far as their locomotive organs are concerned? If so, the prohibitions would apply to imperfect, hybrid creatures such as winged insects that walk on four feet; reptiles that creep on land; crustaceans, batrachians, and mollusks, which cannot swim; and so on. The principle of distinction at work in the cosmogony of origins would, on this hypothesis, recur here, virtually unchanged, in the humblest of dietary practices. One would have the right to eat the world, but only on condition that one remains faithful to the rule according to which the world itself has come from the hands of the Creator: the rule of separation.

In any event, the rabbis' major concern lies elsewhere; their obsession with separation is, generally speaking, of a different kind. To eat what the Gentiles eat is to become like a Gentile oneself. *Kashrut* imposes strict limitations on shared meals between Jews and Gentiles. It seems likely that this is its purpose: to preserve the identity and cohesion of the group and thereby, perhaps, to ensure that it accomplishes its mission outside the group. One does not eat the other's food so as not to become the other. "You shall therefore make a distinction," says God, "between the clean four-footed animal and the unclean, and between the unclean bird and the clean; you shall not bring abomination on yourselves by four-footed animal or bird or the different reptiles with which the ground teems, which I have set apart for you to hold unclean. You shall be holy to me; for I am holy, I am the Eternal, and I have separated you from the other peoples to be mine."[44]

This said—and the whole paradox lies here—not eating the other's food does not prevent one from imitating it. Jewish culinary culture has never cut itself off from its environment. Not only has it always had to strike a compromise with the basic foodstuffs provided by the local market, but it has also adopted many of its non-Jewish neighbors' specialties, while adapting them to the demands of *kashrut*. North African Jewish cooking is also North African, just as Polish Jewish cooking is also Polish. And one typically sweet Turkish dish, whose ingredients include milk and chicken, was served on the tables of Ottoman Jews as well, with just one difference: the Jewish version used coconut instead of chicken! One doesn't eat the other's food, one makes it one's own. . . .

You must not do as they do in Egypt where once you dwelt, nor may you do as they do in Canaan to which I am bringing you; you must not follow their laws.

—Leviticus 18:3

The other is indispensable, and this for at least two reasons, involving flexibility as well as rigidity. There must be a relative other to allow exchange, alliance, and circulation among the different species of our common humanity. But there must also be an absolute other who allows me to pose myself by opposing myself and to remedy the disturbing porosity of my being. The first other is real, present; it is my fellow man, who questions me. I invent or imagine the second; he is everything I am not. He serves to tell me what I am, to respond to the doubts that I might entertain as to what I am.

Biblical thought and rabbinical Judaism have obviously never ceased to secrete this imagined other. The reason is that Judaism has defined itself, to a large extent, as a "counter-religion." It constructs itself and conceives of itself in confrontation with an *external* enemy that is, however, simultaneously a standing *internal* temptation: idolatry.

After filling the Bible with furious and sometimes bloody episodes, the idolatrous peoples have continued to haunt the Jewish imagination down to the present day. There are Ur and Chaldea, the idolatrous lands from which Abraham (whom tradition makes the son of a dealer in idols) had to wrench himself free in order to devote himself to the one God. There is Egypt, a land of slavery, whose sovereign and gods would ultimately be punished and annihilated, a land from which the people descended of Abraham would eventually tear itself in order to dedicate itself to the worship of the unique God, even if it often stumbled and relapsed into the errors of the past. There is Amalek, a cowardly, noxious people if ever there was one, which treacherously attacked the Hebrews just after they left Egypt; henceforth it would be Israel's imperative duty to blot out its memory from under heaven. There are the Ammonites and the Moabites, who, when Israel was en route to the promised land, did not come forth to meet it with bread and water, but bribed Balaam, a Gentile prophet, into execrating it. There are the peoples of Canaan with their abominable practices, the unclean first occupants of the Promised Land; any alliance with these peoples, destined for annihilation, was prohibited. There is Babylon the sinner, the haughty temptress, who destroyed Jerusalem for the first time in 586 BCE and deported Judah far from its own country. There is Edom as well, descended of Jacob's brother Esau, who would soon be identified with the pagan Rome which destroyed the Second Temple in the year 70 of the Christian era, and then with Christian Rome, which persecuted Israel during its millennial exile.

Doubtless all the idolatrous nations are not absolutely confounded by the Biblical and, later, Jewish imagination in an indistinct, irrevocably hostile mass. It was to be remembered that Egypt was not just a land of oppression, but, first, one of welcome and rescue. The Edomite was not to be held in abomination, because it was not to be forgotten that the Edomites were a fraternal people. It was to be recalled that, on a divine inspiration, the Persian Cyrus, a kind of Gentile Messiah "anointed" by the Eternal, freed the Judeans from their Babylonian exile and urged them to go back to their country to rebuild their sanctuary there. As for Christian Rome, it was no longer possible to declare it absolutely idolatrous once Christianity was clearly acknowledged to be a monotheism; it was even harder to condemn Ishmael as idolatrous from the day it accepted Mohammed's message. The more time went by and the further history advanced, the harder it became to conceive of Israel as standing alone against the rest of the world. There were not many who, because they were neither Christian nor Moslem, refused to recognize Abraham's grandeur and were unwilling to be blessed in him in accordance with the prophecy in Genesis: "in you all the peoples of the earth shall be blessed."[45] Where, then, were the last true idolaters? Maimonides, in the Middle Ages, relegated them to "the remote corners of the earth"; they were "the heathen Turks in the far North and the Indians in the far South."[46] Did they really still count?

Yet, as alterity and absolute negativity, or, at least, as an *idea* of alterity and absolute negativity, idolatry is crucial to the self-definition of Judaism. At the same time, it is its major temptation. It is archetypally incarnated in the episode of the Golden Calf, when the Hebrews, tired of waiting for Moses, who had remained up on Mount Sinai, chose to make themselves an ersatz god, an idol. In rabbinical Hebrew, idolatry has a name, or, rather, two. First, it is known as "worship of the stars and constellations," because the worship of the heavenly bodies is regarded as paradigmatic here. The idolater in fact reveres creatures instead of the Creator; he reveres several of them and needs to see them, hence to represent them. Idolatry is constituted by polytheism and representation. Judaism, in contrast, is worship of the one God, with Whom no image is ever associated. But there is another term for idolatry: *avoda zara,* "foreign religion." This is because idolatry is first of all the worship of the other, a form of worship that is other. It is that through which I define the other and against which I define myself. It is that which I must not do and against which all that I do is directed.

Jewish monotheism thus presents itself, first of all, as a triumph over an originary polytheism, a religion that Maimonides, in his *Guide of the Perplexed,* associates with the mysterious people known as the Sabeans. It is precisely this polytheism, according to the philosopher, which many of the stipulations in the Torah aim to combat and eradicate. A wise teacher, God has committed his people to a difficult struggle. The goal is to root out every last trace of the Sabeans' original idolatry and do away with everything bound up with it, "blot[ting] out these opinions from men's hearts," along with anything else that might promote one or another of the practices typical of idolatry: magic, making children "pass through the fire," divination, fortune-telling and soothsaying, sorcery, incantation, necromancy, and so on. The Torah initially served as a tool in the ruthless struggle against the Sabeans' beliefs and customs. Many prohibitions and prescriptions of the Law can be understood only in the light of this combat. It is even, says Maimonides, "the principal and first object of the whole law."[47]

Did the ancient rabbis not teach that those who professed idolatry denied the whole Law and that those who rejected it professed the whole Law?

Are this affirmation of self as a rejection of an absolute, absolutely imaginary other and this definition of the Law as a counter-law still valid today, in a world in which idolatry is no longer all-powerful? They are indeed, for two reasons. First, idolatry is a constant, timeless temptation. Second, imitation of the other, idolatrous or not, is a temptation that the Jews have never totally overcome. Exiled, vulnerable, a minority, inevitably impressed by the material successes and widespread cultural influence of the nations in whose midst they live, the Jews take certain liberties with the principle of separation that informs Judaism considered as a system. They tend spontaneously to believe that the essence of the system will remain intact for as long as the imitations or adaptations in which they indulge do not call this principle into question in an absolute sense. Identifying with their masters, the Jews of ancient and medieval times adopted their languages and drew unreservedly on the abundant sources represented by their sciences and philosophy. We have sufficient proof of this in the abiding fascination that "Hellenism" held for ancient Judaism, as is attested by its Greek translation of the Bible or by writers such as Philo of Alexandria and Flavius Josephus. Medieval Judaism would yield to this fascination in its turn, when the ancient Greek heritage, after passing through the filter of the Arabic language and Islamic monotheism, penetrated Jewish thought, posing new problems and inspiring new syntheses. As for the contemporary period, it has been marked by a host of far bolder attempts to co-opt the other or reduce the distance between it and Judaism. Reform and Conservative Judaism repudiate the stiff, immobile, repulsive norm of an orthodoxy that rejects novelty on principle, on the pretext that anything new ultimately threatens to dissolve Israel's identity in the crazy vogues of the day and the customs of the Gentiles. Feminist Judaism, which sometimes attaches great importance to the principle of strict observance, nevertheless breaks with the ancient distribution of roles and (re)introduces women as subjects at the very heart of the liturgical system and community structure. Gay and lesbian Jews may be attached to the personal and collective manifestation of their twin identities, homosexual and Jewish, even if this means that they must jettison some of the supposedly inviolable rules about sexual distinction decreed by Biblical and rabbinical tradition.

In the eyes of all fundamentalists, the worst and most dangerous form of alliance with the other is, of course, exogamy. Exogamy is apostasy, adultery, and prostitution. It is the dissolution of the self in the other and an unpardonable sin against distinction. "You shall not make a covenant with the inhabitants of the land," God warns on the eve of the entrance into Canaan, "for when they prostitute themselves to their gods and sacrifice to their gods, someone among them will invite you, and you will eat of the sacrifice. And you will take wives from among their daughters for your sons, and their daughters who abandon themselves to the worship of their gods will draw your sons as well into the worship of their gods."[48] This unnatural alliance is a breaking of the alliance with God, the Covenant. The love bestowed on the woman of the other is not merely betrayal of one's own family and people; it is a repudiation of love, infidelity to God himself. At the moment of the return from Babylon, Ezra and Nehemia vigorously reaffirm the prohibition of exogamy and demand that those of the exiles who have violated it send away their foreign wives together with the children these wives have borne them. There is no Biblical precedent to justify the slightest deviation from this rule. Joseph's Egyptian wife? Tradition teaches that she had first sincerely converted to Judaism. Ruth the Moabite, who married Boaz and initiated the lineage that would include David and the Messiah? But Ruth is, precisely, the glorified archetype of the genuine proselyte. If there are foreign women, their foreignness has to be neutralized. It is the other who must yield.

Thus the concern or even alarm of rabbinical authorities and community leaders over the rate of mixed marriages in contemporary Western countries—a rate that sometimes reaches or even exceeds fifty per cent—has deep, not merely conjunctural, roots. It is true that a Jew who marries a non-Jew does not necessarily indicate thereby that he has broken with the community of his birth. New strategies for preserving one's identity are emerging. Reform Judaism makes it easy for a Jewish man to transmit his Jewishness to the children borne him by his non-Jewish wife. But what will be left of all this in the second or third generation, especially if the attachment to Judaism is at best cultural or simply emotional, and less and less religious? Is there not bound to be dilution sooner or later? What is one to think of these "half-Jews," these "quarter-Jews," these new hybrids, neither Jewish nor non-Jewish, who have been brought into the world by modernity? It has been said that to be a Jew is to be Jewish and something else besides. But can this "something else besides" be reduced to an "almost nothing," to a "je-ne-sais-quoi," to the infinitesimal, immeasurable difference of the "psychological Jew" whose social life is not Jewish, who does not practice Judaism, who knows nothing or next to nothing about Jewish culture, yet still calls himself a Jew and still "feels" Jewish?

Even if Judaism was never as fertile as when it allowed itself to be fertilized by the cultures among which history decreed it had to evolve, it has always held that certain limits were inviolable. To its most austere defenders, certain renunciations or compromises have always seemed too dangerous. There is always some fundamentalist to preach retreat and withdrawal against the seductions of porosity and the temptation to contemplate oneself in the other as if in a mirror; there is always someone to repeat the resounding, uncompromising Biblical injunction: "you shall not bow down to their gods, or worship them, or follow their practices."[49] Do not imitate them!

Israel must remain Israel and must struggle against an enemy still worse than the external other: the internal other. For example, the Samaritans,[50] whom the Judeans accused of being nothing more than the descendants of Babylonian immigrants transplanted to Samaria by the Assyrian Sargon; even in accepting the religion of Yahweh, they continued, so the accusation ran, to serve their own gods. For example, the Sadducees[51] of the end of the ancient period, condemned without appeal by the Pharisees and then rabbinical tradition as impenitent scripturalists who deny the immortality of the soul and the resurrection of the dead. For example, the medieval Karaites,[52] who, turning their backs on the whole oral tradition, were accused of depriving Judaism of that which founds and justifies it in order to retain only the empty shell of a Scripture left to the arbitrary interpretation of each individual. There are the Shabbateans as well, disciples of the false Messiah Shabbetai Zevi, who converted to Islam in order to escape the death sentence pronounced against him by the Ottoman authorities. Finally, mention might be made here of the contemporary Zionists who have dreamed—the height of sacrilege!—of making Israel a people like all the others, an ordinary nation, suddenly stripped, in a manner that has scandalized the ultra-orthodox, of its mission and its ultimate, essential singularity.

"Do not follow their practices!" The injunction not only concerns, then, an absolutized other who is entirely other, an imaginary Gentile or idolater against whom Judaism constructs itself. Just as often, it seems to point to a kind of internal enemy, who is no less imaginary, but ambiguous, at once close and distant, with a foot, as it were, to either side of the line. This enemy poses a threat more serious than that posed by the non-Jew. It is the threat of the other born of the same, a sign, were there any need for one, of the indecision or fundamental non-definition of the same. It is a reminder that authentic Judaism does not exist, any more than the wholly other that it invents in order to invent itself. The Jewish figures of otherness are infinitely more alarming than its non-Jewish variant, because they show that distinction is at least as much a lure as a necessity: at best, a necessary lure.

Thus, however one approaches them, all the Jewish strategies of identity seem to culminate in an aporia. Constantly reaffirmed, the ideal of separation and the demand for distinction aim to ensure the persistence of Israel in its own being. At the same time, this quest for permanence mandates compromise and is sustained by negotiation. It is as if one cannot be and remain Jewish unless one is both against and, *simultaneously,* on the side of the other. It is not surprising, in these conditions, that the Jewish ethic itself should bear the stamp of this basic ambivalence, of this salutary indecision. Who, then, is the object of the authentically ethical attitude? Is it the other insofar as he is another self? Or is it the other who is first acknowledged as other and ultimately legitimized as such?

Never seek revenge or bear a grudge toward your kinsfolk; but love your neighbor as yourself. I am the Eternal.
—Leviticus 18:19

What meaning should we assign this injunction? Whom must I love? Is it this neighbor who resembles me, this other in whom God himself is present? "God created man in his image," Genesis tells us, "in the image of God he created him."[53] Emmanuel Levinas expands on this as follows: "In my relation to the other, I hear the Word of God. . . . I'm not saying that the other is God, but that in his or her Face I hear the Word of God."[54] And again, "it is in the Face of the Other that the commandment comes which interrupts the progress of the world."[55] Levinas makes the face, the other, and responsibility for the other the basis of his thought, this "humanism of the other man" whose face calls out to me and to whose appeal I cannot fail to respond, to whose suffering I cannot remain indifferent.[56] Franz Rosenzweig had already emphasized that the love thus enjoined was of divine inspiration. "The love for God is to express itself in love for one's neighbor. It is for this reason that love of neighbor can and must be commanded."[57] The love of one's neighbor, in this case, is nothing more than the worldly realization of the love of God. It is sustained by neither past nor future, but is an "act of love wholly lost in the (present) moment."[58] It is the very existence of the other that calls for this love. "The neighbor is only a representative. He is not loved for his own sake, nor for his beautiful eyes, but only because he just happens to be standing there, because he happens to be closest to me."[59] God and my neighbor are inseparable; each is an integral part of the other, and their presence calls out to me as a particular man or woman present in the world.

But who, let us ask again, is this neighbor? Is it first my near neighbor, the Jewish other, as the context seems to imply? Does the "neighbor" of the Old Testament mean merely "my kinsman"? Must universalization and de-ethnicization of the love of one's neighbor be left to the New Testament, which merely cites the Old? In the commandment in Leviticus, there is a "but" which, when one is attentive to it, indefinitely extends the scope of the love that is commanded. The Talmud will multiply definitions of this "neighbor," effacing his limits, as it were. How could God have created two types of people, the Jew and the other? If it is true that a unique God created a unique humanity, one's neighbor is well and truly present in all humankind.

Thus it is not just a universalistic humanism characteristic of thinkers such as Rosenzweig and Levinas which has put the other at the center of their thought. Scripture and the rabbinical interpretations of it naturally waver between formulating open laws on the Jews' relations to the other and accommodating the circumstances of the moment, which do not rule out rejecting him. Whenever the other is involved, human societies have always hesitated between acceptance and exclusion. Judaism is no exception. In the contemporary period, whenever the Jews have had to adapt to an unrestricted universalism in return for their integration, the ethics of the other—the other other than the Jew [*de l'autre autre que le Juif*]—has inevitably been enriched, and undue attention has not been paid to the asperities in the Jewish tradition that this ethics invoked. Let us not forget that for certain Jewish thinkers of the contemporary period ethics took the place of a declining religious practice, a circumstance that increased its importance and intensified its demands. Not all the asperities, to be sure, were glossed over. Their continuing presence in the Jewish approach to the question of the other simply shows that Judaism is a religion of human beings, with their limitations and ethical demands.

Rea, the "neighbor" of Leviticus, is an ambiguous term. It can mean both the other in the full sense of the word, but also, more restrictively, "kinsman." The scales eventually attain equilibrium, but they also occasionally tilt to one side rather than the other, as when Hermann Cohen gives the word *rea* the modern meaning of "compatriot." Were the Ten Commandments—a sort of charter for living properly in society in ancient times—valid beyond the limits of the group? Did they set out to do more than institute an internal social order? There is no lack of contradictions here. Like other religions and other peoples, Judaism and the Jews had to strike a compromise with the foreigner and take account of the context in order to think their relationship to him and establish the corresponding laws. Depending on whether the Hebrew nation was dominant or dominated, this relationship changed. . . .

Yet Jewish humanism, for its part, always sees beyond the limitations of the moment. In an age in which it is dominant, it is no longer conceivable that the Jew should be the neighbor of just his nearest neighbor, the other Jew. The Jewish humanist looks for proof in Scripture, and he finds it, because it is indeed present there. "The alien who resides with you," Leviticus declares, "shall be to you as the citizen among you; you shall love the alien as yourself."[60] Cohen spells out the broad implications of this commandment. "It was the foreigner who brought the commandment to love into existence. Man was recognized in the foreigner. Love for the foreigner is the original motivation for the love of man."[61] Hence Cohen shifts gradually from the prohibition against taking revenge on one's fellow man, the other Jew, to the commandment to love what he calls human beings in general. He goes on to conclude that "the fundamental law of ethics and therefore, one would hope, of religion as well, is love for everything that has a human face."[62] One must love the other because he is like us, because he resembles us. "We grasp this essential human resemblance much more precisely and powerfully in the case of the foreigner than in that of our so-called neighbor, since 'neighbor', after all, evokes only those closest to us."[63] It is the foreigner who helps us discover the human being. Is this foreign other who is foreign by virtue of his faith and nationality another aspect of the other who is our kinsman? The spirit of Deuteronomy and the Prophets transcends that of the Decalogue. It universalizes the "neighbor." The face of this neighbor is unified; one can no longer distinguish between the "close" and the more distant other, the Jewish and the foreign other. For Levinas, the welcome the Bible urges us to extend to the foreigner is the very content of faith. The foreigner is "one toward whom one is obligated."[64]

The other and the encounter with the other open out onto the infinite. Other people are the infinity that transports me elsewhere and, at the same time, recalls me to myself after this encounter has come about. "I is an other."[65] If to be myself is not to be responsible for the other or answer for the other, what is it? Others not only call out to me, they call me into question and summon me to be just. "It is always starting from the Face," Levinas reminds us, "from the responsibility for the other, that justice appears." This justice makes me feel the suffering of the deprived, the weak, the vulnerable, the mortal. I am responsible for their suffering. "All men are responsible for one another, and 'I more than anyone else.'"[66] God is justice and he is also mercy. And man, who is made in God's image, is laden with, is full of this mercy. "The only absolute value is the human possibility of giving the other priority over oneself."[67]

The other is not simply the other self to whom I am bound not to do the evil that I would not have him do unto me, as Hillel, a sage of the first century, put it. He is also the one whom I must treat with all the compassion called for whenever he is vulnerable. "Cursed be anyone who deprives the alien, the orphan, and the widow of justice."[68] God, who is great, mighty, and terrible, who is not partial, executes justice for orphans and widows and shows his love for foreigners by providing them with food and clothing.[69] Because they are by definition socially vulnerable, widows and orphans, who are associated with foreigners, come in for very special attention in Biblical literature. "Never humiliate the widow or the orphan."[70] Rabbinical Judaism invested this duty to protect and assist widows and orphans with the force of law. Even when they are rich, says Maimonides, they should be treated with the utmost consideration, "because their souls are very depressed and their spirits low."[71]

One of the fundamentals of Levinasian ethics, which is a commentary and a super-commentary on certain basic Jewish texts, a modern reading and re-reading of these texts by a man of the tradition, is the "non-indifference of one to another," the "interhuman" that rests on this "non-indifference. . . . The interhuman is also in the recourse that people have to one another for help."[72] This attitude itself derives from the responsibility one has toward others, without any call for reciprocity. Levinas describes this responsibility for one's neighbor as the love of one's neighbor, "love in which the ethical aspect dominates the passionate aspect." It is a love in which one takes other people's destiny upon oneself.[73] One is reminded of this responsibility by the face of the other; his pain and suffering make an even stronger appeal. "The Ego is infinitely responsible in face of the Other."[74] If the face speaks, as Levinas says, other people's suffering speaks to me as well, speaks to me about myself, penetrates to the core of my individual self, reminding me of my own vulnerability and fragility here and now. Suffering throws my good conscience into turmoil and calls for justice: the justice of the human.

In Hebrew, charity (*tsedka*) also means justice, uprightness (*tsedek*). But another way to say "charity" is *gemilut hasadim,* which signifies exchange and restitution of a good. Generosity and liberality: that is what this "rendering the good," which naturally expects no reward, ultimately comes down to. It is charity as a gratuitous act. The two expressions used to designate charity provide a good reflection of its twofold character. It is a demand for justice and a redistribution of goods, but it is also a spontaneous outpouring charged with humanity. If *tsedka* takes the form of a gift of money, *gemilut hasadim* implies that one should also make a personal sacrifice by visiting the sick or comforting the bereaved. If *tsedka* applies only to the poor, the rich, as well, can be recipients of *gemilut hasadim.* If the former kind of charity benefits the living, the latter is addressed to the dead, too; the acts of homage rendered them are in effect "true goodness," *hesed shel emet,* with no hope of reward. "The death of the other," says Levinas, "challenges me and calls me into question, as if the possibility of my indifference to this death, which is invisible for the other who is exposed to it, made me an accomplice to it; as if, again, even before being doomed to it myself, I had to answer for the other's death and not abandon the other, alone, to his mortal solitude."[75] The vulnerability of the other who is still alive, his vulnerability in the face of death, makes a claim on me and questions me; it is by thus calling me into question that the other becomes my neighbor. The death of my neighbor solicits this "brotherhood amid extreme separation."[76]

It is everyone's religious and moral duty to practice charity; as the liturgy of the Yom Kippur fast reminds us, charity even has expiatory value and can cancel the rigor of the divine decree. At the same time, along with worship and the study of the Torah, it is what the world rests on. As in the other monotheisms, it is not left to the discretion of individuals, but is institutionalized. Biblical law already drew attention to the situation of the poor and humiliated; many of the provisions of agricultural law in the Bible aim to guarantee them minimal protection. Rabbinical Judaism, for its part, makes recommendations as to the way in which the individual should go about fulfilling his obligations: it urges him to be discreet, friendly, and compassionate. It also defines the limits within which charity should be exercised—between one-fifth and one-tenth of a person's revenue, no more and no less—so as to ensure that the necessary assistance will be provided without jeopardizing the economic security of the donors. Above all, it sees to it that the various communities are endowed with institutions capable of mitigating the immediate effects of the most blatant social inequalities. Maimonides stipulated that every city with a Jewish population should establish a charitable fund and an institution to supply the needy with food. Throughout history, Jewish communities have funded various charitable organizations for the purpose of providing impoverished young women with dowries, distributing clothing, caring for and visiting the sick, ransoming captives, helping orphans, providing poor children with an education, and offering lodging and aid to traveling Jews.

The institutionalization of charity was an expression of compassion for the other, but it was also elevated to the level of a charter of justice, one that was particularly valuable for a semi-autonomous social minority, such as the Jews were before they gained the right to citizenship. Although modernity has certainly not done away with the duty to perform charitable acts, it has made it less onerous and has more clearly identified it as a social obligation that is largely taken in hand by the state, thus definitively stripping it, in the eyes of many Jews, of its specifically religious character. In such a context, even if the obligatory exercise of charity is less and less an act incumbent on the individual, the ethics of the other reveals itself to be a still more urgent necessity. In our modern societies, it is precisely when men and women melt into a faceless totality that gratuitous generosity toward the other, without the least expectation of rec-

iprocity, imposes itself on us as an absolute ethical necessity—over against an indifference that leaves us
blind to the other's suffering, deaf to his appeal, and
dumb before an insistence that has neither voice nor
countenance. It is here that the ethics of the other, as
conceived by Levinas in the wake of his predecessors,
(re)invests Judaism with its full significance. Man (or
woman) is responsible for man (or woman). Man is
responsible for the world, for its suffering and mo-
ments of madness, because he is responsible for everyone. One must pass from the human or the universal
to Judaism, and then, with Judaism as one's point of
departure, make one's way back toward the other, in
a to-and-froing that transcends tolerance and is neither a law nor a social convention, but the very basis
of the human.

One arrives at this humanity as if one were landing
on a shore, in the responsibility of each for the other.
But it is a humanity that reveals itself only to those
who await it and, resolutely open to it, adopt a welcoming posture. It involves responsibility and hospitality, like that shown by Abraham, who is sitting
alert at the entrance to his tent, and is prepared, when
three men suddenly appear, to welcome them into his
home, wash their feet, and give them food and drink.
Hospitality, then; and, soon, responsibility. For these
men are on their way to Sodom. And Sodom is
doomed to destruction for its wickedness. Abraham
intervenes without a moment's hesitation. He pleads,
before God, the cause of the few just men who, because they live in the unjust city, may perish together

with it; although they have done no wrong, they risk being swept up in the punishment to be meted out to the sinners. Hospitality and responsibility, the fundamental virtues of a man who welcomes the human, open out onto the more-than-human. They are the path leading to an authentic encounter with the Divine. Were Abraham's three guests not so many messengers sent by the Lord to inform him of the future birth of Isaac and the destruction of Sodom? By way of these three messengers, did Abraham not eventually enter into a conversation with God?[77]

On each night of Passover, every Jewish household adopts a similar posture of welcome and waiting. This is a celebration of freedom regained, and the hope, for oneself but also for all humankind, of an emancipation to come. The ritual therefore begins with a call: those who are hungry are invited to come eat, those who have no home in which to celebrate Passover are summoned to celebrate with those who do. The door stands wide open that night. Through that open door, it is the prophet Elijah who may enter, the prophet whose coming announces that of another: the Messiah.

4 Numbers

Divisions, Mélanges, Transitions

This people lives apart, it does not reckon itself among the nations.

—Numbers 23:9

Israel is alone among the nations! This solitude is sometimes imposed on it by the nations themselves, in times of denial, humiliation, or confinement. It is also willingly accepted by the Jews themselves, as a secret form of glory, the sign of a mission that has not yet been recognized, a privilege and the mark of their election. It is a solitude that is very often reinforced by their religious and lay leaders with a view to closing the community's ranks against attack from without, preventing internal violations of the law of the group, or securing their own power over the community. It is a painful solitude and also an oppressive one for many Jews, who dream of escaping it. When doubt or, simply, religious indifference has taken hold, when it seems as if, in the end, any truth is as good as any other, or when the other's truth asserts itself, resplendent and persuasive, why persevere? What point is there in enduring so many frustrating constraints and privations? A late thirteenth-century or early fourteenth-century Ashkenazi text states the matter plainly enough: apostasy is infinitely tempting![78]

Why not finally become the other and have done with it? Why not eat everything that one craves, revel in the fleshly pleasures of drink and fornication, cast off the yoke of the celestial kingdom so as not to have to be afraid of anything, throw over all the commandments, give oneself up to sin and the delights of this world, and no longer fear for one's life? Why not leave the house of slavery for the one where everything is allowed, moving from darkness to the light? One has to be very strong or very weak to resist so many temptations. Many were to yield to them, going over to the other side, the other's side. Over against the genealogy of the faithful martyrs whom Israel glorifies and vaunts and whose memory it exalts, over against those who preferred death to treason and sacrificed their wives and children with their own hands rather than see them caught in the perverse trammels of idolatrous priests, over against this broad expanse of luminous justifications, there stands a dark, haunting figure who obsesses the collective imagination: the apostate.

There is, first of all, the merely unsettling, ambiguous figure of the apostate for a day, a month, or a few years. Faced with violent persecution—the fury of the Crusaders in 1096, the Spanish populace in 1391, or the rampaging Cossacks of the Poland and the Ukraine of the mid-seventeenth century—or with lesser perils such as the threat of expulsion or extortion, this particular breed of renegade simply sought, in panic, to save his skin or his property. In more peaceful contexts, he might have been just a man of small faith seeking to escape his hard lot and allowing himself to be taken in by either the maneuvers of Christians only too happy to save a soul or the entrancing charms of some lover from the other side. He might, finally, have been a defenseless child who had been torn from his family's arms and dragged to the baptismal font. It was not always easy to tell if such an apostate had wholeheartedly converted or had repudiated his religion under the burden of a constraint too heavy to bear. The Church itself occasionally hesitated to recognize him as a full-fledged Christian. Under certain circumstances, it might authorize him to return to the faith of his fathers. But it might also do quite the opposite, stubbornly insisting on locking him in its embrace and persecuting anyone who tried to facilitate this new apostasy.

The Jews themselves, those, that is, who kept their faith, adopted contrasting attitudes toward those who abjured it. Not all of them had the courage of a Judah

Halevi, who, in Alexandria in 1141, actually risked his own life in the attempt to persuade a former co-religionist who had converted to Islam to follow him to the Holy Land, then under Christian rule, and, there, turn back to Judaism in perfect safety. Not all of them exhibited the audacity and humility of the Spanish Jews who welcomed repentant *conversos* with open arms. Thus many Jews in eleventh-century Germany and France, and, later, in Poland as well, were not far from thinking that baptism had a real, indelible effect. The fact that Rashi, the great medieval exegete, read the Talmudic formula "even though [the people] have sinned, they are still [called] 'Israel' "[79] in a sense favorable to repentant apostates, or the fact that a good many of his successors interpreted the law the same way, was not enough to convince the majority of their flocks to accept the repentant converts without hatred or fear. Should one encourage the returning apostate? Was he to be trusted? Was such a person not, taking him all in all, a traitor? Did one not run the risk, by welcoming him back all too complaisantly, of bringing the ire of the church hierarchy or the state down on the whole community and paving the way for interference in its internal affairs? Should one not rather abandon him, without losing too much thought over the matter, to the wrath of the non-Jews whenever they demanded that he be turned over to them? At the least, should he not be advised to go into exile—if he was, say, Polish, then to settle elsewhere than in Poland, in the dominions of the Grand Turk, for example? Had he truly done penance? How was he to be purged of his sin? Was he still marriageable? Was any member of his family still marriageable? Was it not better to have nothing to do with such people?

Forgiveness was not readily extended to one who had erred, even if only briefly—to one who, by crossing the boundaries, had threatened to efface them. What, then, was to be said of someone who insisted on living in error, who put himself in the service of the other for good and all and became the avowed foe of those he had left behind? An apostate of that kind was a much more sinister figure. Jewish history and the Jewish imagination have painted him with the blackest of features. Did Israel, indeed, have a worse enemy? Let us recall, among many other examples, Saul of Montpellier, the famous thirteenth-century renegade who, after changing his name to Pablo Christiani, was to spend the better part of his days persecuting Jews and attacking rabbinical literature in Spain, Provence, and France in hate-filled polemics. It is as if, either thanks to some strange curse or as punishment for its myriad sins, Israel itself were condemned to forge the perverse arms, so to speak, that its persecutors went on to use against it. It is as if the enemy were already there, within; as if the other had inevitably to loom up out of the same.

In fact, all those to whom rabbinical tradition denied the benefits of the world to come were both Jews *and* renegades, Jews who had betrayed Judaism. There were those who claimed that the Torah did not teach the resurrection of the dead or that it was not of heavenly origin; the Epicureans and the readers of heretical books; those who recited magic spells over wounds; those who dared to pronounce the ineffable Name of God; the sinners who led others into sin; the informers, those who cut themselves off from the community, and, finally, the sectarians. All were known as *meshummadim*. The tradition did not mince words: they were "apostates."

Talmudic literature provides an archetypal, emblematic figure of this kind of apostasy, bestowing a highly revelatory nickname on this adversary come from within, an implacable enemy of himself and his people: Aher, which means, precisely, "the other." Aher was Elisha ben Avuyah, one of the best-known sages of his generation, who, at the turn of the second century, abruptly went over to the camp of the despised Romans. What gave rise to this terrible destiny, this act of treason? It may have been the indirect consequence of a mystic experience, a dangerous contemplation of the Divine. It is said that four sages managed to make their way into Paradise. Only one came back out safe and sound; another died; a third went mad. As for Elisha, the fourth, he directly attacked the roots of being and faith, becoming a renegade. But it is also said that what overwhelmed him was perhaps less the sight of heaven than that of the world here below and the humiliations and tribulations inflicted daily on the very people who know, respect, and teach the principles of the divine Law with utmost conscientiousness. Was Aher, however, unaware that the suffering of the just in this life is made up for by their reward in the next? Still other accounts point the finger at the circumstances of his birth or the principles of his education. When his mother was pregnant with him, the story goes, she came too close to the idolaters' temples and inhaled too much of their baleful incense. His father is supposed to have encouraged him to devote himself to the study of the Torah for the sake of the prestige this would earn him, not for love of the Torah itself. The fact is that Aher, the Jew-become-other, suddenly turned against the very learning that he had pursued all his life. He is said to have put to death any student he saw succeeding in the study of the Law, or to have dissuaded the most promising young people from studying it by urging them to take up worldly professions. Still worse, he used his knowledge of the Torah to help the Romans reach new levels of sophistication in their persecutions of the Jews.

This condemnation of apostasy in the person of Elisha ben Avuyah remains, however, ambiguous. What is condemned is the use to which he put his knowledge, the reality and depth of which are never denied. His disciple, Rabbi Meir, one of the architects of the Mishnah,[80] remained loyal to him, continuing to drink at the fountain of knowledge that he embodied—even when Elisha transmitted this knowledge to him on the *shabat,* which he simultaneously profaned by riding his horse on that holy day. And although God himself seemed to have forever shut the doors of repentance before him, because he had come to know God's power and rebelled against him, Rabbi Meir never lost hope that Elisha would be saved; he was happy to see that he died, after an illness, in the midst of a sob. Was it a sob of remorse? What is more, Rabbi Meir enjoined God himself to let Elisha into the world to come. "Despite his heresies," he declared, "Elisha must be saved for his knowledge of the Law."[81] Thus, in the last instance, Elisha the apostate, the persecutor of Israel, owed his salvation to his learning. It is as if, at bottom, he had never succeeded in crossing the frontier for good and all; as if Aher had, in the end, never become wholly other; as if his abandoning the community had not irrevocably excluded him from it; as if this other engendered within Judaism itself could always, despite everything, despite himself, find hope of redemption in Judaism. It is as if Rashi were still right, even about the worst of the apostates: "though [the people] have sinned, they are still [called] 'Israel.'"

Thus, appearances notwithstanding, it would seem that the realm of the other will never be truly accessible to the Jew: in the eyes of his own people, at any rate, he will continue to be, as it were, the prisoner of an irreducible self-sameness. Yet even non-Jews, or, in any case, some non-Jews, can accept this idea, as if, in *their* eyes this time, no apostasy could ever efface a Jew's Jewishness; as if, in certain contexts, only one principle counted—the affirmation that the border between the other and the same is fixed and can never be crossed. History, however, has never ceased to contradict that principle. No border is inviolable. The epic of the Marranos, vagabonds of identity, masters of hesitation, inventors of spaces of a third kind, provides a magnificent illustration.

Marrano, *converso,* new Christian: these words refer to the same phenomenon. Often pejorative, they were used of Jews who had converted to Christianity in the Iberian peninsula. A popular explosion of rage against the Jews broke out in Seville in June 1391 and spread rapidly throughout the country. Many perished; others went over to the dominant religion. From then on, Judaism was abandoned by more and more of the faithful. But exactly what did these different names designate? Was what was involved not a multifaceted phenomenon?

"Marrano" comes from Arabic and means "that which is forbidden." Initially, the word was an insult thrown at Jews and Muslims who had converted to Christianity. "Marrano" also acquired the meaning "pig," an animal that Jews and Muslims are forbidden to eat. The term finally came to designate specifically those Jews who, after becoming Christians, had remained true to their original faith despite all. Neither *conversos* nor new Christians necessarily practiced one or another form of Judaism in spite of the fact that they had converted, but they did leave one religion for another. Did they, with time, become strangers to the one as well as the other? Or did they remain on familiar terms with both? Did they clearly choose the one over the other, even while remaining outwardly faithful to their new religion? As for the

Marranos, criticized from the first for practicing their Jewishness in secret, were they truly Jews for the Jews, even while they were considered bad Christians by their adoptive group? How did these men and women with their multiple, fluid identities evolve in their own and others' eyes, living as they did at the end of the medieval period, which set great store by firm, clear-cut allegiances?

Suddenly, the other became constitutive of these identities in tension, which blurred borders to the point that one no longer really knew who the other was—to the point that one wondered if one was not the other oneself. This duality made the *converso* what he was, whether he was a sincere convert to Christianity, practiced Judaism in secret, or took his distance from both religions at once in order to escape the unbearable dilemma of alterity. Whatever he did, he came from one space and moved into another; in the process, curiously, he created a third. Late Zionist ideology sometimes claimed that the fifteenth-century Marranos were completely immersed in their Christian identity, and at other times maintained that most of them remained attached to Judaism. Both contentions sell the reality of the matter short, blithely ignoring the ambiguity of these *conversos* in the service of a simple-minded cause, Zionism. On the first thesis, the unshakable attachment of the Marranos to Judaism, one that often cost them their lives, demonstrates the unalterable nature of Jewish identity and the strength of Jewish national instinct.

On the second, the Marranos' wholehearted espousal of Christianity simply shows that life in the Diaspora ineluctably leads to assimilation.

How, in these complex identities, can one sift that which is Jewish from that which is not? Their modernity resides in this very indecision, which consists in being both here and elsewhere, from here and from some other place. Mobility and interpenetration weave definitions of the self that subvert religion and the practice of it. The Marranos who were good Christians were never safe. Their critics kept an unwavering eye on every one of their acts capable of betraying their Jewishness. Even an excess of zeal on their part awakened suspicions. Anything could betray the other in them, even in those who adhered to their new faith without reserve. As for those who really did continue to practice some form of Judaism, in what sense were they still Jews after a few generations had gone by, when their ties to other Jews had become so loose as to be non-existent, especially after the expulsion of 1492? The Marranos of Portugal, forcibly converted en masse in 1497, undoubtedly remained attached to the vestiges of their Jewishness longer, even if these became steadily more uncertain. But the point is that they drifted away from normative Judaism, gradually devising, for their own purposes, an ad hoc Jewishness which was in fact a specifically Marrano identity. Could they still be considered Jews by Jewish Law? Foreigners for themselves, foreigners for the Jews, what were they, exactly? They were foreigners for the Christians as well, who refused fully to integrate them into the Christian matrix.

What was this religion of the Marranos, a secret religion cut off from its vital sources and maintained in the face of the hostility of the outside world? At times, the Inquisition conferred an identity on its victims, making *conversos* who had been assimilated to Christianity (back) into the Jews they had allegedly always been. At other times, nostalgia and a sense of guilt drew certain converts back toward a "Jewish" identity that they experienced in the privacy of their homes. For these converts, there was an inside and an outside, and a semi-rupture with a Christianity sometimes embraced for several generations back. Their espousal of "Judaism," a few altered Jewish rites aside, sprang initially from rejection of Christian dogma and practice, as well as from a firm sense of belonging, like all the other Jews, to the people of Israel, who worshipped the one God and were waiting for the Messiah.

This was a hopeless quest for a lost elsewhere, a quest for a remote goal, an often unconscious quest that was not really defined or formulated. It was dissatisfaction in motion, a hesitation to choose just one of several different worlds, an impossible reconciliation with the demands of a medieval culture dominated by Christianity and a reformulation of new modes of being that defied fierce social and religious control. . . . We too are these Marranos, in a new, individualistic context and a world caught up in the process of globalization. Our difference is not forced on us, but, if we do not want to lose ourselves in an anonymous crowd, our equilibrium depends on it. The Marrano is that other who is very close to us, although he is no longer clandestine. He is an other who calls out to us.

The Israelites shall camp each under his own standard, by the emblems of his father's family.
—Numbers 2:2

The Israelites were to live together and yet separately, each according to his lineage. One's paternal tribe offered a sense of belonging that was at once a specific identity and nostalgia for the lost other. The Messiah will not appear until the two kingdoms, Judah in the south and Israel in the north, are once again fused into a single entity. Jewish consciousness is haunted by this search for the other self, who is very similar and, at the same time, very different. Judah lives in expectation of its brother Israel. Today's Jews are the descendants, it is said, of the tribes of Judah and Benjamin. But they bear the name of Israel, the other who is absent and yet present. And they have given the name of Israel to their new state. Lost or found again, the Jews' other self pursues them. Were the ten tribes of Israel who were long ago deported to Assyria lost forever? The Jews have, rather, chosen to live forever with the memory of the loss. Israel is never whole and never forgets it. Elsewhere, beyond the borders of the known world, on the other bank of the Sambatyon, other descendants of Abraham, Jacob, and Isaac are perhaps living with no memory of their Jewishness. Sometimes it is believed that they have been rediscovered in one place or another; sometimes they are imagined. Yet they are not present, these lost tribes, which have been lost forever—so that the search for the other will never cease.

Ashkenaz and Sepharad were also to look for each other without every really finding each other again. Both the European North, speaking a Judeo-Germanic language, and the South, the Mediterranean South speaking a multitude of tongues, are descended of Judah; yet they refuse to acknowledge a common ancestry. They have two different horizons. The horizon of exegesis is that of the Talmudists of the North. The South's horizon is that of philosophy and the sciences. Rashi's North and Maimonides' South constitute two different crossroads, two different modes of thought. The bards are from the South, as are the thinkers steeped in Arabic and Latin culture. The North hews to the Law, and is, perhaps, more austere. Yet, for a long time, Sephardic culture also shaped Ashkenazi thought, and vice versa. For thought circulates; and if men do not, books, at least, do. This permeability blurs contours; it puts Ashkenaz and Sepharad side-by-side, and both does and does not exclude their face-to-face confrontation. For they are divided by geography, by flavors and colors, by the Christian hosts of the one and the Muslim hosts of the other, as well as by words, gestures, knowledge, and customs, even if these things also unite them around the same Book and the same Law. Beneath one and the same roof, walls often prevent encounters.

On the one hand, there was Ashkenaz, which Talmudic sources identify with Germania. It extended its borders East and West, as the various migrations and persecutions dictated. Sepharad, in medieval Hebrew, simply designated the Iberian peninsula, the land in which the Jews rubbed shoulders with Islam and Christianity. Their descendants went into exile after being expelled from Spain in 1492. They scattered throughout Europe, Northwest Africa, and the East. They were extremely proud of their origins: were they not of David's line, like the future Messiah? Over the course of a long history, Sepharad extended its dominion. Soon the term "Sephardim" would be applied to all who were not Ashkenazim and had, more or less, the same rite in common—a rite polymorphous enough to take in a vast zone stretching from the two shores of the Mediterranean to the frontiers of Central Asia. From the Maghreb through the Middle East to the Balkans, everyone called himself a Sephardi. The term was imprecise, in view of the great variation within the Sephardic world. It was likewise unjust to bring Ashkenaz, as vast and multifaceted as it was, under the umbrella of a single term. No matter—the need to simplify prevailed. Yet a simplification this certainly was. A Jew from Leghorn might, citing his Iberian origins, refuse to be buried in the same cemetery as his Tunisian co-religionist, who, with his North African background, was not

"Sephardic" enough for him. Everyone invoked the "purity" of his lineage. Nothing was more alien for a Jew from North Africa than a Sephardi from the Balkans. What separated them? The cult of alterity. The Sephardim who could trace their origins to Spain devised hierarchies tailored to their purposes. The natives of Istanbul made fun of their neighbors from Adrianopolis; as for those who hailed from Salonika, were they not, as they saw it, the most aristocratic of the aristocrats? They were, certainly, Iberian; but they were aristocrats besides. Nothing was simple in this Sephardic Tower of Babel. And what shall we say of the Ashkenazi Babel? The twists and turns in the labyrinth of Ashkenaz were no less serpentine than those in the labyrinth of Sepharad. Being a *litvak,* a Lithuanian Jew, was more than a matter of origins. It was a sign, or, at least, a respected form of intelligence. . . . Ashkenaz embraced German Jews, Polish Jews, Russian Jews, and so on and so forth. A particular region enjoyed, or claimed to enjoy, more prestige than another. Every city had its Jews, but not all Jews were alike. Was one neither better nor worse than the next? There was no unity; diversity and division were the warp and woof of Jewishness.

The Jews of Edom, children of Christian lands, peer over a wall at the Jews of Ishmael, who hail from the domain of Islam. If, even in the same cultural space, every Jewish community uses a particular pejorative term to refer to its sister communities, where does Jewish unity reside? For, despite their cultural differences and multiple origins, the Jews do, after all, think of themselves as one. Their unity is constituted by these particularisms, which, to be sure, are not always fraternal. They do not find it impossible, with all these differences, to think of themselves as a unified whole. Israel's identity is woven of such differences, of the diverse landscapes in which its experience has unfolded, of these many different implantations that have made the Jews what they are. How are we to love ourselves, beyond a common Judaism that can, of course, unite us, although not always—indeed, far from it, given the great diversity of its forms? The encounters between Jews, perhaps, pass by way of encounters between men and women involving more than their common religion. And these encounters take their place on a continuum with another, earlier encounter, that of the Jew and the other in his world outside. For it was there, in the land of their birth, in another clime, the foreigner's, that, beyond their Judaism, the Jews acquired their experience of humanity. Ashkenaz and Sepharad are two worlds, two climates, two cultures, two profoundly different elsewheres; and there is a plurality of different beings in each.

The plural was born in dispersion; the unity of Israel was constructed in the singular. The bridges between these singular differences were built as the course of history dictated. Sepharad inspired Ashkenaz with its openness, its taste for rational speculation, and its education, which held out the promise of modernity. The men of the Jewish Enlightenment took Sepharad as their model, as an illustrious, valued precedent, in their struggle for progress. Eager for integration into non-Jewish society, the Jewish West sought inspiration in Sepharad, in its Golden Age and its values. A mythologized Sepharad suited the purposes of Ashkenaz, which was elaborating its new myths. Sepharad's prestigious past on Iberian territory, the glory of its statesmen, the integration achieved by its Jews, its poets and thinkers—all helped bring Sepharad closer to Ashkenaz in an imaginary fraternity. The time of forgetting came later. Sepharad was conflated with a backward-looking Islam. It was no longer a model; it returned to its place as other, as an other stripped of its finery.

Like the West as a whole, the Jews of the West set out to discover the East, the elsewhere par excellence for a nineteenth century bored by its contemplation of itself and thirsting after the exotic. They rediscovered their co-religionists in the remote lands of Islam. The orientalist vogue was in full swing. In these colonialist times, everyone had his favorite barbarians. The West set out, with missionary fervor, to civilize the lands it had conquered. Its motivations were noble. It needed justifications. Like the others, the Jews were not slow to take up their civilizing mission. The Western Jewish press described, at great length, the Jewish populations of the East, who wore traditional dress and still paid tribute to the customs of a bygone era. They were set in an imaginary landscape. The childhood of Western Judaism was projected onto these Jews who were thought to be of another age. Bittersweet nostalgia for the lost paradise of the period before emancipation was conjoined with pitying condescension. The time had come for the Jewish institutions spawned by integration to take these disinherited brothers under their wing and bring them up. Schools were opened and the Jews of the East were taught the language of civilization, French. Their culture, their languages, their way of life, all were marked out for improvement. The gaze of the colonizer was not wasted on trivialities. The noble savage had to be brought out of the darkness that enveloped him. The Sephardim belonged to yesteryear. They were the Western Jews' now antiquated other, the other whom they contemplated with a touch of sadness but wanted, when all was said and done, to do away with, so that there would remain only one valid model of the Jew, the Western one. It was the arrogance of the rich toward the poor, and it spelled humiliation for the poor. The Easterners began to dream of the remote but envied West, which remained inaccessible for many of them. The humiliated then struck out on the path of Jewish nationalism, a more tangible dream for the Jews who had been shunted aside by Westernization. Zionism began to bud in these circles. But Zionism too was a child of the West that looked down on the Jews of the East.

Israel, the country whose mission was to gather all the exiled together in a unified nation, created still more exiles within its borders. Each diaspora settled into its own particularism on this promised land of reunification. They were supposed to speak a single language and constitute a single nation: the dream foundered on the sands of otherness. Even the natives of the new country still bore within themselves the distant memory of their lost origins, without ever succeeding in permanently melting into the unity that had been imagined for them. The line of demarcation still ran between North and South, dividing them more fiercely than ever before. Ashkenaz wore the aura of the builders; Sepharad bore the stigma of populations that had been brought in to people the new nation. Yet neither Ashkenaz nor Sepharad was ever to constitute a compact, unified entity. There were different classes of citizenship for the deserving Israelis and the others, and differing forms of treatment for a population that did not divide up the manna equally. The milk and honey of the dreamt-of promised land did not flow with the same abundance for everyone. Sepharad smacked of the Arabs. The fact that some Sephardim did not come from Arabic countries was forgotten. They were branded Easterners. They were the people from the East, meaning the Muslim East. Exclusion grew out of this conflation of the Easterner with the Arab: exclusion from the camp of the privileged, the educated, the Westerners, of those who had inherited the benefits of "civilization." A kind of colonial view of the situation relegated the Easterners to the world of the "barbarians," those who did not speak Yiddish, the language of the Ashkenazim, the only language that provided access to the authentic, valorized form of Jewishness. Salvation hailed from *Yiddishland*. In the language of the *shtetl*, of the little Jewish town lost somewhere in

Eastern Europe, the one used by the tellers of tales in a now vanished Jewish world, the Easterners were known as the *shvartze,* the "Blacks." In Palestine, and, later, in Israel, the Sephardim, who were allotted the hardest jobs and lived for many long years in the tents of the camps of transit, would never forgive the builders of the new nation for the inferiority that they reaped in the guise of a salary.

Black: that is also how the Jews of Europe were described in the ethnological literature of the late nineteenth century. Black was the mark of the Jews' inferiority and a sign of their sickliness. The West regarded its Jews as Blacks. In their turn, the Sephardim became the Blacks of the European Jews. The Black was the other par excellence. The Sephardim suffered from their Sephardity: it was a disease that was hard to shake. Black was not beautiful. The Sephardi was a Jew who was other. In Israel, he incarnated, for a long time, otherness conceived as cultural difference and cultural deficiency. He would hear a pejorative remark here and a jibe there. Soon, however, the situation was turned around: the inferiority to which the Sephardim had been relegated was organized as a political force. In the beginning, there were the black panthers. Then came the slap dealt to the left, which had made no secret of its contempt for the Sephardim from the day they arrived; this slap brought the right to power in 1977. Today, the situation is colored by religion and the politicization of religion. While their culture had not been recognized, their religiosity and traditionalism, at least, had been, although these were not always to the taste of the founders of the state, who were socialists and partisans of a secular political system. From now on, the Sephardim would proclaim their loyalty to tradition and transform it into political ferment. The Moroccan Jews, the most disreputable Sephardim in the Second Israel, seized on this ferment, harnessing it to the cause of a party, the Shas. But the dream, even for them, remains, paradoxically, a dream of Ashkenazicity. Irrevocably, they have taken up their positions on the other side of the line, that of the ultra-religious right. Religion, their sole weapon, is perhaps not the most effective one with which to combat the Whites, the other Jews, those who belong to the Establishment and have taken the biggest piece of the pie. Are they, then, the Jews' Jews? Or, quite simply, Jews?

In France, too, in Yiddish-speaking circles, the Easterners were the *shvartze*. These were the North African Jews who arrived in the 1960s and revitalized the Judaism of a country bled white by the end of the war. They had brought the sun in their suitcases and they carried it about with them in a country whose skies are often heavy with rain. The sun does not prevent anyone from shining. In France, in front of others, the *shvartze* assume their difference, which they sometimes publicly proclaim and sometimes do not. In France, they are not exactly the other Jews, because they form the majority and, in the eyes of non-Jews, are first of all Jews. Their dazzling success, their numbers, the position they have attained in non-

Jewish society somewhat attenuate their "négritude," which they experience differently than in Israel.

But there are not only those Blacks. There are also the men dressed in black: the ultra-orthodox. Here is another line of demarcation. When religion was at the foundations of society—of Jewish society as well—degrees of religiosity did not constitute criteria of separation. Religion was common to one and all, and tensions did not rule out co-existence. The crises of modernity overturned the old order. The eighteenth century, a period of oppression, persecution, and rampant poverty, saw the flowering of a mystical movement, Chassidism. It put a premium on religious spontaneity and had soon incurred the wrath of normative Judaism, which met it with excommunication. Another current took shape, that of its opponents, the *Mitnagdim,* who criticized the Chassidim for putting prayer above learning and denounced them to the Russian authorities for heresy.

In the nineteenth century, the advocates of the Jewish Enlightenment refused to discriminate between these two movements, taxing both with obscurantism. Jews who are other, other Jews, see their numbers swell whenever Jews are no longer compelled to follow silently in the steps of their community. The possibility of breaking into non-Jewish society offered them new perspectives. The Jews' religiosity developed on distinct, staggered levels. The seeming unity of the Jewish world was fragmented. There were now anti-religious Jews, moderately religious Jews, ultra-religious Jews, secularized Jews, Jews who had forgotten or were trying to forget their Judaism, Jews who wanted to reform Judaism, Jews who had withdrawn in order to flee a world that had become too agitated for them. The issues were confused, spaces were redefined and redistributed, alterities were intensified. Lines were drawn and positions hardened; loyalties were superposed and, often, counterposed.

Who, then, is the real Jew? Is there a Jew who is better and more authentic than the others? Who perpetuates Judaism? The fragmentation induced by modernity has redrawn the Jewish map, so that an ultra-orthodox Jew is, for a secularized Jew, more alien than a non-Jew. Moreover, certain attitudes toward Jewishness are determined independently of all reference to religion. The ways of being a Jew are spontaneously invented and combined as people's needs and expectations require. Might there be several Judaisms? Or can each individual be a Jew in his own fashion? How can one accept a Jewish other altogether different from oneself, while also accepting oneself as both different and similar? Dialogue, whenever it is interrupted, stimulates or even imposes a new creativity. New combinations engender new forms of cohesion around lines of fracture. Retreats, flights, returns, revisions: all go to make up Jewish being today. From these ruptures and interrogations, there are emerging new rituals or secular cults such as that devoted to remembering the Holocaust, which is supposed to play a unifying role: there exists a new Jewishness based on commemoration of the tragedy. But is that Judaism viable over the long term?

Convergent and divergent Jewish alterities are laying the groundwork for a Judaism of the future: an uncertain Judaism, but, perhaps, a rich one. The gap between the ultra-religious and the secular, which weighs ever heavier on Israeli society, is, however, fraught with danger. It is gaining ground in the Diaspora as well. Aggressive alterities divert us from the real problems. Only an alterity that is accepted in a face-to-face confrontation with universalism and only a universalism that tolerates diversity can create the indispensable space for a dialogue among the various components of Judaism, of a Judaism open to the world, not one in retreat from it.

5 Deuteronomy
Antagonisms and Reconciliations

Bear in mind what Amalek did to you.

—Deuteronomy 25:17

In the traditions of Deuteronomy that were later taken over by the prophets, the covenant between God and Israel is the founding paradigm of Judaism. When destruction rains down on the Jewish people, the reason is not at all that it has been abandoned by a God negligent in the performance of his duties or that it has been eclipsed in the competition with the other forces of the universe. God is present and the destruction must be regarded as a punishment commensurate with Israel's sins. Indeed, this punishment even becomes an expression of his continuing interest in his people insofar as its suffering ensures the expiation of the sins that brought on the punishment and allows the survivors to re-establish their relationship with God. In the tragedy of Israel's downfall, its enemies are confined to the role of intermediaries chosen by God to punish its iniquities; once they have served their purpose, they too are struck down. Their chastisement is the more severe whenever they exceed the limits of the divine plan and punish Israel more harshly than was necessary. Thus the antagonism between God and his suffering people is mediated by the presence of an enemy who had previously been conflated with God. From now on, the enemy comes forward as a distinct figure who can be made to bear the burden of Israel's bitterness. It is precisely his existence which makes reconciliation between Israel and its God possible.

Yet both Israel and God have another, radical enemy who poses a threat, a terrible one, to the people's very existence. Amalek, Esau's grandson, is his original, absolute, emblematic incarnation. He is the first enemy Israel meets after crossing the Red Sea. Joshua wages war on him, and, with Moses' blessing, vanquishes him "with the edge of the sword."[82] "And the Eternal said to Moses: 'Write this as a reminder in a book and recite it in the hearing of Joshua: I will utterly blot out the remembrance of Amalek from under heaven.' "[83] Yet Amalek is by no means destroyed. The memory of his perfidy forever haunts the consciousness of the Jews. For he launched his assault on the stragglers, attacking Israel from behind at a time when the people, having just torn itself from Pharaoh's clutches, was exhausted, at the end of its strength. Amalek, for his part, does not fear God. It is because he goes so far as to assail the throne of the Eternal that war must be waged on him to the end of time: "from generation to generation!"[84] His name becomes a symbol: Amalek is the enemy par excellence.

Haman, the minister of Ahasuerus, king of Persia and Media, is the archetype of the anti-Semitic persecutor and the first man, if we credit Biblical sources, to have planned a massive extermination of a dispersed Jewish population. Fortunately, his plan was foiled by Mordechai and Mordechai's cousin Esther after she had become Ahasuerus' wife. Haman was a descendant of Amalek's.[85] Even if the dating and historical reality of the events recounted in the Book of Esther are still matters of controversy, they are commemorated every year in the Jewish world on the holiday known as Purim. Many Jewish communities were later to institute local Purims in order to preserve the memory of other occasions on which, they thought, Jews had been miraculously saved from destruction. Purim is a holiday of exile that recalls both danger and the always real possibility of being saved; it provides an occasion for all sorts of merry-making, one of which takes an oddly cannibalistic form, with the preparation of special pastries such as Haman's "ears" or "pockets." The enemy is symbolically ingested: this renders him harmless and is a consecration of the victory gained over him. Thereafter, he is inside, not outside.

But it is not only those who want to destroy Israel who are the enemy. It is also those who reject, imprison, or humiliate it. The enemy is anyone who rejects the Jew as other—and the enemy is the other who rejects.

In Christendom, this rejection was initially theological. The Jews were people who had neither acknowledged Jesus as the Messiah nor recognized his divinity. Converting to Christianity might begin to gain them acceptance, but only at the price of their disappearance. This disappearance was not, it should be added, universally desired, because the survival and continuing existence of the Jews, faithful guardians of the Book, counted as a proof of the Christian faith. As for the subaltern status to which they had to be confined, it was both punishment for their blindness and a sign of the authenticity of Christ's message. But the gradual marginalization of the Jews, which went hand-in-hand with the rapid expansion of Christianity, led to their demonization: a demonization that crystallized and intensified the hatred of which they were increasingly the targets. Soon the Jew had come to embody Evil. It was an Evil that could contaminate those who came too close, and it required that all the forces of Good be marshaled against it. The Jew was now a diabolical, accursed creature whom the Christians did everything in their power to stigmatize, ostracize, and expel. The mythical figure of the wandering Jew surged up naturally in the imagination of the "sedentary" Christian. Wandering was the punishment meted out to a whole people, the latter-day Cain, for the crime it had committed against Christ. It was a people that now lacked ties and roots and that existed by virtue of this lack. Reworked time and again, the myth made its way down to the end of the nineteenth century. The modern wandering Jew, decked out with distinct signs, continues to haunt people's imaginations. It sometimes happens, as well, that he is metamorphosed into the cosmopolitan Jew, the exotic Jew, the Jew from elsewhere, the pariah of modern times, unrelentingly targeted by anti-Semitic broadsides. His wandering has become consubstantial with his being. It is the destiny of his "race."

The laws about the purity of the blood that began to obsess the Iberian peninsula at the end of the Middle Ages institutionalized a new kind of discrimination between Christians of pure-blood and those others who, as descendants of Moors, heretics, or Jews, were forever marked by the impurity of their origins. In an ideal society, even some of the lowliest tasks were supposed to be effected by none but pure-blooded Christians. Blood was to provide a new criterion for making the necessary distinctions. The newcomers to Christianity were eternal prisoners of their genealogy. Whether they were the children, grandchildren, or great-grandchildren of the converts whose memory had haunted the Spaniards ever since the fourteenth century, whether they had taken the path of Christianity because they had been forced to or because they had thought they must, all of them fell irrevocably into the category of the impure. As such, they were excluded, marginalized, driven beyond the social pale. This obsession with the pure and the impure would survive into the nineteenth century. The host of rules and regulations governing selections based on "blood" was not abolished until 1773 in Portugal and 1860 in Spain.

Inspired by the anti-Judaism of the Middle Ages, modern anti-Semitism spread like an epidemic throughout a Europe that had now set off on the race for progress. In the imaginary scheme of the new era, the Jew continued to be perceived as a living compendium of all existing crimes and threats. He was identified as the ultimate cause of all the problems besetting a transitional society that sought to rid itself of its tensions by discharging them on him. Spontaneously, he became the target of the aggressive forces spawned by change and a focus for the resentment of all who had been left on the scrap heap. These powerful, widespread anti-Jewish feelings were easily transformed into political weapons in the hands of ideologues eager to erect a new order. That is how the Nazis proceeded. The Jew, the absolutized other, was soon metamorphosed into the racialized other. A number of eighteenth-century and nineteenth-century "scientific" theories made his "blackness" a subject of debate. His color betrayed his racial inferiority and sickly nature. He was black and, consequently, the other par excellence. Was the Jew's Jewishness, then, a sort of disease? This marked the shift from symbolic discrimination between pure and impure to physical, hygienic discrimination between black and white, the healthy and the pathological. Now the pure became white, and the impure, black. Because the Jews were "dirty," they naturally aroused feelings of rejection. Being black, at the time, also meant being ugly. The Jews' blackness was the sign of just how different they were. Were they not more closely related, when all was said and done, to the Africans than to the Europeans, who, in this, the heyday of colonialism, arrogantly proclaimed their superiority? To the blackness of the Jewish character were added the marks engraved on the Jews' flesh and visible in their faces: for example, the famous "Jewish nose." Many Jews, prisoners of the images forged by their enemies, did indeed hope to improve their noses (surgically!), imagining that this would enable them to improve their position in a society that assigned them limits they could not overstep.

In the 1946 *Portrait of the Anti-Semite,* published in the aftermath of a conflict that brought the extermination of six million Jews, even Jean-Paul Sartre describes one of his Jewish friends in terms that would not have been disavowed by the very anti-Semites on whom he had declared war: "When I was living in Berlin, in the early days of the Nazi regime, I had two French friends, one of whom was a Jew and the other not. The Jew represented an 'extreme Semitic type': a hooked nose, projecting ears and thick lips."[86] Sartre adds, "However that may be, and even while admitting that all Jews have certain physical traits in common, it is not possible to conclude from that, unless by the vaguest of analogies, that they must therefore all possess the same traits of character."[87] "The slightly hooked nose [and] the protuberant ears"[88] seemed to him to be typically Jewish, although his aim was precisely to avoid reducing the Jew to a caricature. Curiously, then, the Jew as anatomical other emerges from descriptions penned by an intellectual who can hardly be suspected of the least hostility toward the people he is describing.

Is Jewishness, then, indelibly engraved in the flesh, so that neither assimilation nor denial of one's origins is capable of effacing what cannot be effaced? Do the Jews' thick lips inevitably exile them from the West, insensibly bringing them closer to Africa? The Jews were people of another clime and race; their culture might breed illusions, but not their features. Thus, after the racial categories of the nineteenth-century had become things of the past, together with the race laws of the period of the War and Occupation and the anti-Semitic descriptions and caricatures that stigmatized the Jews by mocking their supposed physical traits, the Jews continued to display, in the gaze of the other, the marks of the dissimilar, even in the immediate wake of the conflict and its disasters. Stamped as other to the point of caricature, the Jews became aliens even in their own eyes. Thus Sartre contended that "it is not the Jewish character which provokes anti-semitism, but, on the contrary . . . it is the anti-semite who creates the Jew."[89] The Jew's very Jewishness was the work of the other. This was the supreme denial of his own identity: he now depended entirely on the other's gaze, on that disapproving gaze which went so far as to bring him into existence through the very negation of his own being.

Trapped in the role of an other who was at once absolute and indistinct, the Jew, too, imagined his other, the "non-Jew." This non-Jew, called a "Gentile" (a word rather more innocuous than not) in refined French, now became the "goy." In the Bible, "goy" simply means "people" or "nation," often, although not systematically, in contradistinction to "Israel." In the rabbis' parlance, the term came to refer to any non-Jewish person, even acquiring a feminine form, "goya." Usage invested it with pejorative, rather unfriendly connotations. There are, to be sure, goys and goys. Moreover, the Jews' goy was obviously not strictly analogous to the anti-Semites' Jew. He could even be assigned positive functions. Thus, in traditional Jewish societies, one could find many familiar, everyday representatives of the indispensable, non-hostile other. There were the *shabes goys*:[90] the Jews of Central and Eastern Europe used to ask them to perform certain tasks that they themselves were prohibited from carrying out at any time during the weekly day of rest, such as lighting or extinguishing lamps or a fire. There were the non-Jews to whom the orthodox Jews, then as now, used to sell, on the eve of Passover, all the food that they were forbidden to eat or possess until the holiday was over; of course, they would buy it back from them a week after selling it. There were, as well, the non-Jews, Muslims in this instance, who, in the Maghreb, traditionally brought their Jewish neighbors their first fermented meal after Passover, thus marking the beginning of the very popular festival known as Maimuna.[91] The other was relegated to the realm of the forbidden, yet he simultaneously helped the Jew to avoid violating the Law. He reinforced his Jewishness and allowed him, in one and the same gesture, to display his difference while sealing an alliance with the different.

The feminine version of the non-Jewish other, the goya, inspired, in her turn, the most contradictory fantasies. In Yiddish, she came to be called the *shikse:* the forbidden but fascinating woman, whose offspring, from a strictly orthodox standpoint, could not ensure the continuity of a Jewish line. *Shikse* comes from the Hebrew word *shekets,* which means "abomination" in Biblical Hebrew and is associated with the impure and the soiled. But the *shikse* is also a seducer; the Jewish imagination has managed to fit her out with the most beguiling charms, which possess all the allure of the forbidden. This particular other is unsatisfied desire. She is strangely analogous—for once, the analogy holds—to the Jewish woman as perceived by the non-Jew. She too is powerfully seductive: she is a dreamt of, terrifying otherness. In the works of Christian painters, she is incarnated in Biblical figures: Eve the temptress, Deborah the warrior, the cruel Judith, the bloodthirsty Salome, all of them portraits of a desired, inaccessible, feared woman. Literature too gives these women their due. In the nineteenth century, they continued to exercise their seductive power in novels in which they figured as courtesans and prostitutes, women of the sort one did not marry, although they fanned the flames of desire and provided the bourgeois household benumbed by its comfort what it lacked in the way of forbidden pleasures. These Jewish women were associated with the East, an imaginary place in which all pleasures and fantasies were permitted, in the freedom of the exotic and the far-away.

Otherness was refracted in innumerable ways. If, in Christendom, the goy was the figure of the other par excellence, the Arab or Muslim enjoyed similar status in the Islamic world. Here too, color indicated where the other stood. In the Ottoman Empire, the Muslim Turks took their name from the color of Islam. Green, *Vedre,* was what they were called in the privacy of Spanish Jewish homes. Was the Turk still considered a fellow creature, a human being, another self? He was the other color. As for the Arabs in both Turkey and, later, Israel, they would be associated with the color black. Jews were black for Western non-Jews; Sephardim were black for Ashkenazim; for Jews, Arabs too were black: *Preto.* The color black cast you out of the realm of the human and swallowed you up in a vision, a look, an imagination that classified things and nature as it saw fit. In the multi-ethnic Ottoman Empire, in which relations between the non-Muslim communities were fraught with tensions of all sorts, even Armenians were given a name that associated them with the animal world. They were called *Ratones,* rats. As for Greeks, another minority engaged in fierce economic competition with the Jews, they were "the people who never smile." They lacked the smile, that which makes human beings human.

The pioneers who stepped ashore in Palestine in the early days of Zionism wanted to adapt to a land that had long enjoyed mythical status. They intended to work the land so as to make it more fully a part of themselves. But, to become the land's, they also had to appropriate the customs and clothing of the natives, which meant, in this instance, the nomadic Bedouins. This time, the other would be co-opted. Thus it was that young Russian Jews, and intellectuals to boot, could suddenly be seen wearing local dress. Photographs of the period show them decked out in garb that it would be hard to imagine today. And their mimetic ardor did not stop there. They also tried hard to eat what their models ate. The (re)construction of a Hebrew identity thus proceeded, paradoxically, by way of imitation of the identity of the other—or, at any rate, what seemed to be his identity. In this case, the other was the Bedouin.

For the founders of political Zionism did not, in contrast, always pay heed to the sedentary Arabs who had from time immemorial inhabited the lands they coveted. Quite simply, they did not see them. They refused to see them. As the Zionist enterprise developed, the tensions between the two peoples steadily mounted. The creation of the state and the Arab defeats of 1948 and 1967 only widened the abyss of hostility between the defeated, dominated Arabs and the Jewish conquerors. On the Israeli side, the 1973 Yom Kippur War reinforced the idea that the stake of this conflict was the very existence of the Israelis' state. And, with every passing year, the two peoples who were settled on the same soil became further estranged. They were enemies and foreigners for each other; yet they were also united, if only by their common desire to live on that land.

It was precisely at this point that Amalek reappeared. In the discourse of many right-wing Israelis, the Arabs are the new Amalek. The invisible other has become the absolute enemy, the enemy who intends to annihilate you, the one with whom no compromise is possible. From this point on, an implacable hatred was to legitimize, in the eyes of certain people, the principle of total war. For the war against Amalek—against the Arabs—is a just, necessary war (*milhemet mitsva*). Since October 2000, the second Intifada has brought a long string of murderous terrorist attacks and acts of brutal retaliation, sowing destruction and desolation on both sides. Decades of reciprocal delegitimization of the other have rendered his sheer presence intolerable. The other is simply seen as a radical threat of destruction. He must himself be destroyed. Each party to the conflict dons, by turns, the murderer's costume and the victim's. The media cannot really account for this perverse spiral of violence. The Middle East will find it very hard to recover from this apparently absolute abandonment of the ethic of the other. Hatred for the other, when it becomes as intense as this, is obviously suicidal. It is patently so in the act of the terrorist who sacrifices both his own life and that of others. It is doubtless no less so, although this is not as easy to see, in a certain Israeli irredentism. Peace can only spring from the recognition that the other is one's true fellow man. Real peace, which is peace with the other, is also peace with oneself.

Peace with oneself, however, is exactly what modernity seems stubbornly to refuse to grant the Jew. . . .

Among these nations you will find no repose . . . the Lord will give you an anguished heart, dim eyes, and a dismayed spirit, and your life ahead of you will hang in doubt.
—Deuteronomy 28:65–66

Are the Jews from somewhere else? Or are they simply given to understand that they are not from here? And are they not ultimately tempted to think so themselves? This confusion, which prevents those who feel it from accepting themselves, is not inevitable, but it is, after all, quite common. Other people beside the Jews have also, because they are of a different color, gender, sexual orientation, or religion, suffered from an absence of love that can, under certain circumstances, degenerate into hatred or persecution. And other people beside the Jews, who were expecting love, and sometimes did all they could to be deemed worthy of it, have also ultimately been led to internalize the rejection of which they were the victims.

In the nineteenth century, in western Europe,

emancipation and integration opened up new paths before the Jews. They now considered themselves capable of entering modernity on an equal footing with everyone else and of becoming avid participants in the forward march of civilization. It was as if nothing could stop them. At last, the road was open. Apparently, nothing would now set them apart from the other citizens of the countries that had adopted them and given them, as never before, the chance to improve their lot. Yet transcending what made them different was also a challenge, especially now that they at last had the means to do so.

In central Europe, those who took up this challenge went to extremes. The first steps had been taken by cultivated, polyglot Jewish women from rich families; they had opened the doors of their salons to everybody who counted in the societies of their day, building a bridge between Jewish and non-Jewish elites in an effort to pave the way to mutual comprehension. These *salonnières* of the late eighteenth and early nineteenth centuries, women steeped in the ideas of the Enlightenment, looked confidently to the future. Following the ideals of the German Jewish Enlightenment, which took much of its inspiration from the *Aufklärung*,[92] they abandoned their customary roles and embodied the process of individual integration that the new situation made possible for certain privileged people.

Yet their cultivation, knowledge, and good manners were not by themselves enough to make others forget their Jewishness. The ultimate act of integration, marrying aristocratic non-Jews, enabled them to attain full-fledged respectability at last. No longer considered Jews, relieved of the burden of the past, they ended up seeking the road to individual salvation in Christianity. Exogamous marriage and conversion: such was the tribute required of this first generation of women determined to transcend the limits of their condition as women and as Jews. They lacked the time to forge a plurality of identities, as later generations would, amid the complexity that is the very substance of Jewish modernity.

Once they had been integrated culturally, the Jews of central Europe spared no effort to win the confidence of their compatriots so as to obtain legal recognition of their equality. Yet states were often slow to grant legal recognition of their full, unrestricted emancipation. Although they moved in step with the culture of their day, these Jews were, so to speak, moored to the banks of an otherness that negated their entire being and continued to deny them access to the realms to which they aspired. Invisible borders still reminded them of their Jewishness and curbed their social ambitions. They espoused the culture, values, and language of their countries of residence. They ultimately became producers of this culture, while remaining avid consumers of it. Freed of the medieval restrictions that had kept them isolated, they rushed to join the ranks of the cultivated middle classes. They came forward as active patrons of high culture, went to plays and concerts, owned paintings and libraries, and provided their children the most refined humanist educations available.

The whole culture of the *Aufklärung* had been governed by the ethos of *Bildung*,[93] an ethos of education and self-cultivation. The German Jews, who had to wait for emancipation for a long time but whose educated classes had long since set out on the path of integration, were among the most enthusiastic partisans of this ethos. Their devotion to it made sense. They expected it to engender a neutral society, a cultural and social space in which their religious affiliation would no longer put them at a disadvantage. But it was not long before the ethos of *Bildung* was itself pressed into the service of constructing a specifically German collective identity. Nationalism appropriated it for its own purposes while betraying the values underlying it. The Jews were the only ones to continue to believe in these values. *Bildung* had functioned as a secular religion that did not condemn them to apostasy. Pluralism would have been possible in a society founded on *Bildung*. That society never came about.

Those who could not learn to accept this isolation could still drape themselves in the other's religion. They were in the unbearable situation of having to adopt a religion under constraint and for the sake of convenience: a religion that they had not chosen, but that served as their "ticket" to dominant society. This dualism, dictated by circumstances, was ultimately as oppressive as the Jewishness that they had not been able to leave behind. As for the others, they continued to maintain their Jewishness with their secularity, a Jewishness that was the harder to assume in that it was not associated with a faith or religious practice. It was an abiding sign of difference, at least in others' eyes, in a situation in which a creeping anti-Semitism was making itself ever more strongly felt. Many had believed that this anti-Semitism was a passing thing, because it was unjust. But it gnawed away at the very roots of Jewish being. The Jew was still the unloved child of the societies in which he lived. He did not really understand why. Was he still capable of loving himself?

The concept of Jewish self-hatred was first formulated in the late 1930s by Theodor Lessing. The drama he wrote about had been engraved in his flesh, and he knew what damage it could do the Jewish soul. It was, moreover, by no means a concept that he applied to the Jewish situation alone; it seemed to him to be valid for the rest of the human race as well. In his view, the trajectory of the modern Jews, which led from the hatred to which they were subjected to the internalization of this hatred, simply provided a particularly apt illustration of self-hatred.

The central European Jew suffered from the incompleteness of his condition and was, sometimes, humiliated by it. The rejection he met at the hands of the other, whether imaginary or real, engendered a vulnerability that activated his hatred of his Jewish self. It was a hatred of the group to which he belonged despite himself; and, despite himself, he had to share the opprobrium that this group was made to bear. How was he to live as a modern individual under this burden, which nothing came along to diminish? This Jewish self-hatred could become so unbearable that self-annihilation seemed the only way to escape it. The suicide of Otto Weininger, a famous Viennese philosopher who had converted to Protestantism, furnishes an extreme illustration of the impasse into which Jews were driven: they could no longer endure the eminently negative image reflected back at them by a society riddled with anti-Semitism, even as they continued to internalize that image.

More frequent in nineteenth-century and twentieth-century central Europe, this pathology was also, for many Jews, a translation of their feelings of guilt for having betrayed their Jewishness without ridding themselves of it in others' eyes, even after a conversion. Hence these Jews were plunged into a world without hope: what awaited them was voluntary or inevitable exclusion from the Jewish world and the world of the non-Jews alike. They experienced this exclusion as an absolute split, but no viable alternative presented itself to them. Lessing, who invented the concept of self-hatred, claimed that there did not exist a single person with Jewish blood in his veins in whom one could not make out at least the beginnings of it. The Jew is not at home anywhere; yet he thinks that his place is in the host society which he has consciously chosen, even if it has never really accepted him. His disillusion is the more bitter in that he no longer has any means of rejoining the ranks of the society he came from, since it too has become alien to him.

The unloved Jew was more or less condemned to being unable to love himself. An increasingly virulent anti-Semitism redoubled this absence of love and the terrible suffering it caused. Yet self-hatred was not an inevitability or a constant in the biography of modern Jews. It was subject to variations, often vanished altogether, and was sometimes even transformed into its opposite. Some learned to come to terms with this fractured existence, this rejection by an other from whom they had hoped to obtain recognition in the form of a well deserved gift that he refused to give them. For a few, voluntary or even voluntaristic adhesion to the stigmatized group into which they had been born offered, despite all, one possible escape from humiliation. The path leading back to the womb was, however, littered with obstacles, and no small ones at that.

The poet Heinrich Heine, who tried to make a place for himself on both sides of the line, between Protestantism and a Judaism that he never entirely effaced, imagined, in a prophetic vision, a new Jerusalem born of the encounter between Germans and Jews. These two ethical nations would, he declared, at last create the new Jerusalem . . . on the banks of the Rhine. This was a transplantation, to the territory of the other, of the thrice holy city of Judaism: the city of the holy word, of pure spirituality, and of prophecy. Heine's was the dream of an artist who hoped that he could at last reconcile the Jewishness he had abandoned with the Christianity he had "conquered." Later, Franz Rosenzweig, too, would turn back to Judaism, while dreaming of a Germany that would be a land of two rivers, a new Aram-Naharayim, a new Babylon, a land of confluences, the reunion of the Tigris and the Euphrates. It was in Babylon that Judaism had had its hour of glory, erudition, and wisdom, and had seen the emergence of the Talmud. Yet the dream of a Jew steeped in German humanist culture and capable of inventing a modern Judaism would be shattered: shattered the dream of the new Babylon; shattered the dream of a dialogue initiated by Jews who, without wishing to cut themselves off from their cultural heritage, treated it, in their hope of achieving symbiosis, as the object of a possible exchange. It was the rise of Nazism that shattered this dream.

In France, of course, the situation was different. The fact that the Jews had acquired citizenship even before achieving full integration led others to take a view of them which, while not without detours and gaps, was less convoluted. But the fact remains that the Jews' desire for symbiosis with the larger society they lived in did not inevitably result in assimilation. The ways in which they negotiated their identity were manifold. It was possible to be a convinced partisan of the republic and yet remain a Jew, even while adopting French values. In the new context then beginning to take shape, the creation of plural, many-layered identities was one response to life in the Diaspora. How harmonious the result was depended on the nature of the space opened up by the host society as well as the situation and politics of the states concerned. Extremist alternatives were not lacking: one could take refuge in one's Judaism or simply throw it over for another religion. As a rule, it was the other embodied in society as a whole and its capacity to accept pluralism which determined the choice. Extreme tension with the other sometimes led the Jews to internalize the hatred directed against them.

Self-hatred is a product of modernity. The modern Jew was forced to choose. He had to pick his way among the multiple identities offered to him in a configuration quite different from the one that had prevailed earlier, when he was firmly bound to his group. His contacts with the outside world were no longer governed by a limited number of strictly codified rules, while his relation to his own Judaism was no longer dictated by fidelity to a genealogy that he might earlier have considered immutable because of his beliefs.

As soon as he came into existence, the modern Jew had to find a way of managing the conflict that pitted his traditional self against a self eager for change. By force of circumstance, a transition was made from the "we" to the "I," from membership in a collectivity to individual self-affirmation. In eastern Europe, the Jews did not achieve emancipation in conformity with the Western model; only tiny elites, not the group as a whole, were relatively well integrated into the surrounding society. Autobiography, a genre that blossomed with the advent of individualism, now made its appearance. It retraced the wrenching experiences of the Jews who confronted modernity and, amid nostalgia for the past and a sense of guilt, contemplated abandoning the world from which they had come. Rousseau's *Confessions* set the tone. In the eighteenth century, the *Lebensgeschichte* of, say, Salomon Maimon cleared a path for a form of expression that would soon make a place for itself in Hebrew and Yiddish literature.

The authors of these texts give us an immediate account of their experiences. Autobiographies are written in periods of crisis or change, when the disintegration of certain social and intellectual strata leave people face-to-face with themselves. In the nineteenth-century Jewish autobiographies produced in an eastern Europe traversed by the movement of the Jewish Enlightenment that had been launched in Germany a century earlier, writers described their experiences as orphans, criticized the education that they had received in the traditional Jewish school system, mourned the childhood years that they had wasted in schools run by narrow-minded rabbis, or evoked sexual problems that they traced back to the blows they had received in their infancy. Sexual impotence revealed the uncertainties of egos torn between self and other, the Jew of the past and the Jew of the future. These writers promoted the movement of the Jewish Enlightenment in Eastern Europe; at the same time, they were agents, witnesses, and victims of a transformation. As such, they elaborated an uncompromising critique of a traditional society which they made responsible for all the evils that the Jews faced and their own personal woes as well.

In these autobiographies, personal history spills over into the symbolic representation of an epoch. Fatherless childhoods evoke the precarious condition of the Jewish people, made even more precarious by the gradual destruction of its foundations, hard hit by an ineluctable modernity. To be an orphan was also to suffer the guilt feelings to which anyone leaving his community for the surrounding society is prey. Tortured adolescence and its grave internal conflicts offered an image of the days of anguish and the historical transition that the Jews of these regions were going through. The rootless adolescent who is the hero of these autobiographies incarnated these Jews' lack of identity and their dramatic loss of self. The titles of a number of early twentieth-century autobiographical works reflect this marginality, indetermination, and wrenching division. The feeling of marginality is made worse by the feeling of writing in a vacuum that was common to these authors. They gave expression to a self plunged into a chaotic world, a self made in the image of a social group that had begun to disintegrate. Matters were complicated still further by the identity crises that people were experiencing in their teens and twenties. Sexual impotence and incontinence, which are recurrent themes in these works, underscore the disarray of these men who had to confront a terrifying world, one they were ultimately incapable of bringing under control. This transitional generation voiced its fears by portraying a tortured, split self trapped in a situation of failure, yet inexorably caught up in the course of history as well. Resolutely facing the future, it was nevertheless a generation incapable of mourning the passing of the other, the traditional other which it had not succeeded in eliminating and which prevented it from merging completely with the modern, progressive other it aspired to become. This was an agonizing contradiction in which two selves, having become alien to each other without quite achieving full separation, went on hating each other with an impotent hatred.

Today, the Jews would clearly seem to have overcome these dilemmas. Self-hatred affects Jews less in a day and age in which difference is not proof of inferiority. Jewish is beautiful now. Difference has the place of honor and counts as a privilege for those who lay claim to it. The principle of difference has been accorded official status and institutionalized in a country such as the United States, the inventor of affirmative action, a form of positive discrimination which sets up mandatory quotas destined to create a space of opportunity for ethnic and/or oppressed minorities, as well as women. To be sure, affirmative action is not particularly popular in Europe, or, at any rate, in France, because it stands discrimination on its head without, in the end, challenging the principle it rests on—because it is thought to jeopardize social cohesion by perpetuating separate ethnic communities. Yet, its unpopularity notwithstanding, affirmative action does attest that the reality of the rejection of difference is now being taken into account. That said, it should be added that the Jews themselves are not directly concerned by these laws and regulations, because there can be little question that they have been successfully integrated into the so-called liberal societies. Today, Jewish difference is perhaps not the most disadvantageous or the hardest to live with. This is all the more true in that, after World War II and the terrifying tragedy of the slaughter of the European Jews, Jewish difference is tolerated and handled with a very special tact dictated by the West's guilt feelings, in a day and age in which, at regular intervals, one wave of repentance after another is sweeping over our increasingly moralistic societies. Anti-Semitism does sometimes surface, but it is not perpetuated by states. Today Jewish difference finds expression in this framework. It is no longer necessarily the source of dramatic inner conflicts. Nor is it inevitably charged, as it was in the past, with a negativity capable of sowing all manner of destruction.

In Lieu of a Conclusion

Forgiveness and Respect for the Nations

The Jew as other was not always a victim. The image of the Jew as absolute victim emerges from a re-reading of history in the light of the genocide, in a period in which victims as such occupy a privileged place, since victimization too can be invoked in support of a claim to difference. The Jews are manifestly not the only ones to have joined this trend or to find themselves swept up by it. Moreover, for many, the peoples without land have always represented the perfect victims. Yet it would be a mistake to project the nationalist ideologies of the last two centuries onto the past. Especially in Christian societies, there have existed many different arrangements for managing, in more than acceptable fashion, the problem of living together with Jews, the others par excellence. In the Islamic countries as well, such arrangements have taken many different forms, depending on the period. The Jew as other was not, then, always a victim. For a long time, he was tolerated. Yet his status did not irrevocably cut him off from his environment.

The nineteenth and twentieth centuries saw the Jews enter Western society as citizens. The West allowed them to flourish in its midst, even as anti-Semitism, assuming its modern shape, called their new-found status into question. World War II carried anti-Semitism to a virulent extreme and, in tragic proportions, destroyed European Jewry. Is forgiveness possible? Repentance comes from those who feel a sense of guilt. But forgiveness must come from those who have been wronged.

In this connection, Levinas reminds us of the Talmudic doctrine which has it that, if a man's transgressions toward God are well and truly expiated on the Day of Atonement, his transgressions toward his neighbors are not, unless he has already appeased them.[94] During the great fast of Kippur, the faithful show that they have repented, do penance for their sins, and seek divine forgiveness. God can accord this forgiveness without reserve for the offenses of which he himself was the victim. When it comes to the evil someone has done his neighbor, matters are more complicated. The wronged person must himself grant forgiveness. What if he refuses? What will the person who is not forgiven do? Each finds himself face-to-face with the other, with no possible recourse: not only the one who seeks forgiveness, but also, perhaps, the one who does not want to grant it. Moreover, the offender must want to ask for forgiveness and the offended party must want to bestow it. Even a simple verbal injury is serious.[95] What are we to say of cases in which human beings have lost their lives? "The seeking for forgiveness never comes to an end," says Levinas. "Nothing is ever completed."[96] He goes on to emphasize that there are "two conditions for forgiveness: the good will of the offended party and the full awareness of the offender."[97]

We are very far, here, from "an eye for an eye," the law that subjects the guilty party to a punishment identical to the wrong he has done his victim. The Hebrew Bible offers several different illustrations of this principle: "anyone who maims another shall suffer the same injury in return: fracture for fracture, eye for eye, tooth for tooth; the injury inflicted is the injury to be suffered."[98] We find, in the rabbinical tradition, a discussion of this "measure for measure," which is in fact excess for excess whenever it is strictly applied. The choice that the tradition ultimately settled on was the payment of damages, that is, financial compensation. To put out the eye of someone who has put out an eye only seems just. There is never strict equivalence between the victim's eye and the offender's; the victim may be sharp-sighted, the offender not. And how is one to punish the blind man who has put out his neighbor's eye, the one-armed man who has cut off someone's arm, the maimed person who has maimed another? Nothing ensures that the guilty party who is punished in this way will not be exposed to a danger greater than his sentence called for.

What shall we say of the terrible crime that Europe perpetrated against its Jews? Forgiveness is difficult. Those who might have granted it are dead. There is, furthermore, no punishment commensurate with the crime. And those who did the killing are also dead. Yet Leviticus calls for reconciliation—the reconciliation of the living. "You shall have one law for the alien and for the citizen; for I am the Eternal, your God."[99] These are the very words with which the Biblical statement of the *lex talionis* ends. They are words that put both sides, Israel as well as the nations, under the gaze of the one God. They are words that speak of law, justice, and equity. But they also contain an appeal for peace.

Is to forgive to forget? Should the Jews, can the Jews, forgive the crime committed by those who, only recently, excluded them from our common humanity? Is any forgiveness possible for the absolute immorality of what they were made to suffer? Forgiveness has been asked for—not by the murderers themselves, but by those who, coming after them, have consented to bear the burden of a past wrong. To continue to live without forgetting, while accepting all the demands of a Jewish ethics that both celebrates life and honors the dead—is this not a kind of forgiveness, a forgiveness that does not forget the Jews' immense suffering and remembers it every time that others suffer, whether they are men, women, or peoples? Levinas has said, following Emil Fackenheim: "Jews, after Auschwitz, are pledged to their faithfulness to Judaism and to the material and even political conditions of its existence."[100] Let us add that Jews, after Auschwitz, are pledged to their faithfulness to others and their sensitivity to the suffering of others. At a time when the Near East is daily put to fire and the sword, when the *lex talionis* is making a strange reappearance, there is something to be said for recalling these two truths in tandem. A mutilated Israel and a Palestine bled white are simultaneously destroying their common future.

Genesis tells us that Sarah, Abraham's wife, demanded that he send away Ishmael, the son he had had by Hagar.

> So Abraham rose early in the morning, and took bread and a skin of water, and gave it to Hagar, putting it on her shoulder, along with the child. . . . When the water in the skin was gone, she cast the child under one of the bushes. Then she went and sat down opposite him a good way off, about the distance of a bowshot; for she said, "do not let me look on the death of the child." And as she sat opposite him, she lifted up her voice and wept. And God heard the voice of the boy. And he said to Hagar: "come, lift up the boy and hold him fast with your hand, for I will make a great nation of him." Then God opened her eyes and she saw a well of water. She went, and filled the skin with water, and gave the boy a drink.[101]

In commenting on these verses, the ancient rabbis say that the angels protested when they witnessed this scene; they asked God how he could give water to someone who was destined to make Israel suffer. God is supposed to have answered that he judges everyone for what he is, not for what he is to become. For his part, Levinas, who cites this doctrine, adds: "the eternity of the Jewish people is not the pride of a nationalism exacerbated by persecution."[102] This eternity is achieved beyond such nationalism, amid respect for the nations.

Notes

1. *Midrash* (Hebrew): the classical form of rabbinical exegesis, inaugurated in ancient Palestine and developed in a vast literature that writers in various parts of the Diaspora continued to compile down to the twelfth century.

2. Deuteronomy 33:2.

3. Exodus 33:11.

4. Exodus 33:20.

5. In the Kabbalah, the ten *Sefirot* are emanations of the divine and its first manifestations. They are conceived in opposition to *Ein-Sof,* the "Without-End": that is, the hidden, unknowable, and absolutely transcendent God.

6. Isaiah 45:7.

7. Job 1:1.

8. Job 2:7.

9. Babylonian Talmud, *Kiddushin* 40b.

10. Job 42:3.

11. Genesis 2:24.

12. Emmanuel Levinas, *Time and the Other and Additional Essays,* trans. Richard A. Cohen (Pittsburgh: Duquesne University Press, 1987), p. 85.

13. Ibid., p. 88.

14. Simone de Beauvoir, *The Second Sex,* ed. and trans. H. M. Parshley (Harmondsworth: Penguin, 1972), p. 16.

15. Proverbs 31:10.

16. Proverbs 31:12.

17. Hosea 2:18 and 2:21–22.

18. Genesis 21:12.

19. Genesis 12:1.

20. Jan Assmann, *Moses the Egyptian* (Cambridge: Harvard University Press, 1997).

21. Deuteronomy 6:4.

22. Judah Halevi, *The Kuzari,* trans. Hartwig Hirschfeld (New York: Schocken Books, 1964), p. 79.

23. The phrase is taken from Genesis 22:17.

24. Halevi, *The Kuzari,* p. 216.

25. Moses Maimonides, "Epistle to Yemen," in *Maimonides' Empire of Light: Popular Enlightenment in an Age of Belief,* ed. Ralph Lerner, trans. J. L. Kraemer (Chicago: University of Chicago Press, 2000), pp. 104–106. See also Amos Funkenstein, *Maimonides: Nature, History, and Messianic Beliefs,* trans. Shmuel Himelstein (Tel Aviv: Mod Books, 1997), pp. 61–62.

26. Halevi, *The Kuzari,* pp. 226–227.

27. Moses Maimonides, *Mishneh Torah, Melakhim,* 11:4 (uncensored version), cited in Isadore Twersky, *Introduction to the Code of Maimonides (Mishneh Torah)* (New Haven: Yale University Press, 1980), p. 452.

28. Numbers 15:15–16.

29. Leviticus 25:23.

30. Isaiah 56:8.

31. Isaiah 56:6–7.

32. Deuteronomy 23:8.

33. See especially Leviticus 19:33.

34. Babylonian Talmud, *Gittin* 59b and 61a.

35. Jeremiah 29:5–7.

36. The phrase may be found in *Mekhilta According to Rabbi Ishmael: An Analytical Translation,* vol. 2, pt 7: Neziqin, chap. 18, LXXV: I.1.D, trans. Jacob Neusner, Brown Judaic Studies 154 (Atlanta: Scholars Press, 1988), p. 210.

37. Genesis 11:7–9.

38. Deuteronomy 22:5.

39. Leviticus 20:13.

40. Genesis 2:24.

41. Genesis 4:10.

42. Leviticus 17:14.

43. Exodus 23:19 and 34:26; Deuteronomy 14:21.

44. Leviticus 20:25–26.

45. Genesis 12:3.

46. Moses Maimonides, *The Guide of the Perplexed,* ed. Julius Guttmann, trans. Chaim Rebin (Indianapolis: Hackett, 1995), p. 176.

47. Ibid., p. 145.

48. Exodus 34:15–16.

49. Exodus 23:24.

50. The Samaritans are an ethnic-religious community whose origins are still a matter of controversy. There are only a few hundred representatives of this community left in Israel. The Samaritans themselves believe that they are the direct descendants of the two tribes, Ephraim and Manasseh, which trace their origins to Joseph.

51. The Sadducees formed a political and religious current in ancient Judaism. They were active in Judea from the second century BC to the first century AD.

52. The Karaites formed a current that first appeared in Judaism in eighth-century Babylon. It was characterized by its exclusive attachment to the letter of the Scriptures.

53. Genesis 1:27.

54. Emmanuel Levinas, *Entre nous,* trans. Michael B.

Smith and Barbara Harshav (New York: Columbia University Press, 1998), p. 110.

55. Ibid.

56. Ibid., p. 33.

57. Franz Rosenzweig, *The Star of Redemption,* trans. William W. Hallo (Boston: Beacon Press, 1971), p. 214.

58. Ibid., p. 215.

59. Ibid., p. 218, translation modified.

60. Leviticus 19:33–34.

61. Hermann Cohen, *Jüdische Schriften,* ed. Bruno Strauß, vol. 1 (Berlin: C. A. Schwetschke & Sohn, 1924), p. 188.

62. Ibid.

63. Ibid., p. 189.

64. Emmanuel Levinas, *Difficult Freedom,* trans. Seán Hand (Baltimore: Johns Hopkins University Press, 1990), p. 173.

65. Emmanuel Levinas, *Humanism of the Other,* trans. Nidra Poller (Urbana: University of Illinois Press, 2003), p. 60.

66. Levinas, *Entre nous,* pp. 104, 107.

67. Ibid., p. 109.

68. Deuteronomy 27:19.

69. Deuteronomy 10:18.

70. Exodus 22:21.

71. Moses Maimonides, *The Book of Knowledge: From the Mishneh Torah,* trans. H. M. Russel and Rabbi J. Weinberg (Edinburgh: The Royal College of Physicians of Edinburgh, 1981), p. 46 [*Deot'* 6:10].

72. Levinas, *Entre nous,* pp. 101–102.

73. Ibid., p. 103.

74. Levinas, *Humanism of the Other,* p. 33.

75. Emmanuel Levinas, *Éthique comme philosophie première,* ed. Jacques Rolland (Paris: Rivages, 1998), p. 97.

76. Ibid., p. 98.

77. See Genesis 18.

78. See Jeremy Cohen, "Between Martyrdom and Apos-

tasy: Doubt and Self-Definition in Twelfth-Century Ashkenaz," *Journal of Medieval and Early Modern Studies* 29 (1999): 431–471.

79. Babylonian Talmud, *Sanhedrin* 44a.

80. The Mishnah is a codification of the Oral Law. It was published in Palestine around 200 AD.

81. Jerusalem Talmud, *Hagiga* 2:1.

82. Exodus 17:13.

83. Exodus 17:14.

84. Exodus 17:16.

85. See Esther 3:1 and 1 Samuel 15:8.

86. Jean-Paul Sartre, *Portrait of the Anti-Semite,* trans. Erik de Mauny (London: Secker and Warburg, Lindsay Drummond, 1948), p. 51.

87. Ibid.

88. Ibid., p. 52.

89. Ibid., p. 120.

90. Yiddish for "non-Jew for the *shabat.*"

91. The Maimuna is a spring and fertility festival celebrated by North African Jews. It begins at dusk on the last day of Passover and continues the next day.

92. The German Enlightenment.

93. Education, formation (German).

94. See the Babylonian Talmud, *Yoma* 85a–85b and Emmanuel Levinas, *Nine Talmudic Readings,* trans. Annette Aronowicz (Bloomington: Indiana University Press, 1990), p. 12.

95. Levinas, *Nine Talmudic Readings,* p. 19.

96. Ibid., p. 24.

97. Ibid., p. 25.

98. Leviticus 24:19–20.

99. Leviticus 24:22.

100. Levinas, *Entre nous,* p. 99.

101. Genesis 21:13–20.

102. Levinas, *Difficult Freedom,* p. 201.

Selected Bibliography

Abitbol, Michel. *Le passé d'une discorde: Juifs et Arabes du VIIème siècle à nos jours.* Paris: Perrin, 1999.

Alcalay, Amiel. *After Jews and Arabs: Remaking Levantine Culture.* Minneapolis: University of Minnesota, 1993.

Assmann, Jan. *Moses the Egyptian: The Memory of Egypt in Western Monotheism.* Cambridge: Harvard University Press, 1997.

Attias, Jean-Christophe. "Du judaïsme comme pensée de la dispersion." *Les nouveaux cahiers* 129 (fall 1997): 5–12.

———. "Du prosélyte en monde juif: une impossible inclusion." In *De la conversion,* edited by Jean-Christophe Attias, pp. 37–46. Paris: Cerf, 1998.

———. "Paternité et filiation dans quelques biographies juives de Jésus au Moyen-Âge." In *Proceedings of the*

Ninth Congress of Jewish Studies, Division C: Jewish Thought and Literature, pp. 69–76. Jerusalem, 1986.

Attias, Jean-Christophe, and Esther Benbassa. *Dictionnaire de civilisation juive*, 2d ed. Paris: Larousse-Bordas, 1998.

——. *Israel, the Impossible Land*. Translated by Susan Emanuel. Stanford: Stanford University Press, 2003.

Bahloul, Joëlle. *Le culte de la table dressée: Rites et traditions de la table juive algérienne*. Paris: Anne-Marie Métailié, 1983.

Barnavi, Elie, and Saul Friedländer. *Les Juifs et le XXème siècle: Dictionnaire critique*. Paris: Calmann-Lévy, 2000.

Baskin, Judith R., ed. *Jewish Women in Historical Perspective*. Detroit: Wayne State University Press, 1991.

——, ed. *Women of the Word: Jewish Women and Jewish Writing*. Detroit: Wayne State University Press, 1994.

Benbassa, Esther. *The Jews of France: A History from Antiquity to the Present Time*. Translated by M. B. DeBevoije. 2nd ed. Princeton: Princeton University Press, 2001.

——, ed. *Transmission et passages en monde juif*. Paris: Publisud, 1997.

Benbassa, Esther, and Jean-Christophe Attias, ed. *La haine de soi: Difficiles identités*. Brussels: Complexe, 2000.

——. *The Jews and their Future: A Conversation on Jewish Identities*. Translated by Patrick Camiller. London: Zed Books, 2004.

Benbassa, Esther, and Aron Rodrigue. *Sephardi Jewry: A History of the Judeo-Spanish Community, 14th to 20th Centuries*. 2nd edition. Berkeley: University of California Press, 2000.

Bernasconi, Robert, and Simon Critchley, ed. *Re-Reading Levinas*. Bloomington: Indiana University Press, 1991.

Birnbaum, Pierre. *Sur la corde raide: Parcours juifs entre exil et citoyenneté*. Paris: Flammarion, 2002.

Braude, Benjamin. "Cham et Noé: Race, esclavage et

exégèse entre islam, judaïsme et christianisme." *Annales: Histoires, sciences sociales* 57/1 (Jan.–Feb. 2002): 93–125.

Buber, Martin, *I and Thou*. Edited and translated by Walter Kaufmann. New York: Touchstone, 1970.

Butler, Judith, and Joan W. Scott, ed. *Feminists Theorize the Political*. London: Routledge, 1992.

Bynum, Caroline Walker, et al. *Gender and Religion: On the Complexity of Symbols*. Boston: Beacon Press, 1986.

Cohen, Hermann. *Jüdische Schriften*. Edited by Bruno Strauß. 3 vols. Berlin: C. A. Schwetschke & Sohn, 1924.

Cohen, Jeremy. "Between Martyrdom and Apostasy: Doubt and Self-Definition in Twelfth-Century Ashkenas." *Journal of Medieval and Early Modern Studies* 29 (1999): 431–471.

Cohen, Shaye J. D. *The Beginnings of Jewishness: Boundaries, Varieties, Uncertainties*. Berkeley: University of California Press, 1999.

Dahan, Gilbert. *The Christian Polemic against the Jews in the Middle Ages*. Translated by Jody Gladding. Notre Dame, Indiana: University of Notre Dame Press, 1998.

De Beauvoir, Simone. *The Second Sex*. Edited and translated by H. M. Parshley. Harmondsworth: Penguin, 1972.

Derrida, Jacques. *Adieu to Emmanuel Levinas*. Translated by Michael Naas and Pascale-Anne Brault. Stanford: Stanford University Press, 1999.

———. "At This Very Moment in This Work Here I Am." Translated by Ruben Berezdivin. In *Re-Reading Levinas*, edited by Robert Bernasconi and Simon Critchley, pp. 11–50. Bloomington: Indiana University Press, 1991.

———. *Writing and Difference*. Translated by Alan Bass. Chicago: University of Chicago Press, 1978.

Deutsch, Haim, and Menahem Ben-Sasson, ed. *The Other*. Tel Aviv: Yediot Aharonot, 2001 [Hebrew].

Endelman, Todd, ed. *Jewish Apostasy in the Modern World*. New York and London: Homes & Meier, 1987.

Fram, Edward. "Perception and Reception of Repentant Apostates in Medieval Ashkenaz and Premodern Poland." *AJS Review* 21 (1996): 299–339.

Funkenstein, Amos. *Maimonides: Nature, History, and Messianic Beliefs*. Woodstock, Vt.: Jewish Lights, 1998.

Gallagher, Philip F., ed. *Christians, Jews and Other Worlds: Patterns of Conflict and Accommodation*. Lanham, Md.: University Press of America, 1988.

Gilman, Sander. *Jewish Self-Hatred: Anti-Semitism and the Hidden Language of the Jews*. Baltimore: Johns Hopkins University Press, 1986.

——. *The Jew's Body*. London: Routledge, 1991.

Goldstein, Bluma. *Reinscribing Moses: Heine, Kafka, Freud, and Schoenberg in a European Wilderness*. Cambridge: Harvard University Press, 1992.

Gutoff, Joshua. "Meaning What We Pray, Praying What We Mean: The Otherness of the Liturgy." *Conservative Judaism* 42/2 (winter 1989–90): 19–20.

Hadas-Lebel, Mireille. *Jérusalem contre Rome*. Paris: Cerf, 1990.

Halbertal, Moshe, and Avishai Margalit. *Idolatry*. Translated by Naomi Goldblum. Cambridge: Harvard University Press, 1992.

Halevi, Judah. *The Kuzari: An Argument for the Faith of Israel*. Translated by Hartwig Hirschfeld. New York: Schocken Books, 1964.

Halpérin, Jean, and Nelly Hanson, ed. *Comment vivre ensemble. Actes du XXXVIIème colloque d'intellectuels juifs de langue française*. Paris: Albin Michel, 2001.

Halpérin, Jean, and Georges Lévitte, ed. *L'Autre dans la conscience juive: Le sacré et le couple. Données et débats. Actes des XIIème et XIIIème colloques d'intellectuels juifs de langue française*. Paris: PUF, 1973.

——. *Les Soixante-dix nations: Regards juifs sur les peuples de la terre. Données et débats. Actes du XXVIIème colloque d'intellectuels juifs de langue française*. Paris: Denoël, 1987.

Herzog, Gerta. "The Jews as 'Others': On Communicative Aspects of Anti-Semitism." *Acta*, no. 16. Jerusalem: The Vidal Sassoon International Center for the Study of Anti-Semitism, 1994.

Heschel, Susannah, ed. *On Being a Jewish Feminist*. New York: Schocken Books, 1983.

Israël, Gérard. *La question chrétienne: Une pensée juive du christianisme*. Paris: Payot, 1999.

Katz, Jacob. *Exclusiveness and Tolerance: Studies in Jewish-Gentile Relations in Medieval and Modern Times*. Scripta judaica 3. London: Oxford University Press, 1961.

———. *The "Shabes Goy": A Study in Halakhic Flexibility*. Translated by Yoel Lerner. Philadelphia: Jewish Publication Society, 1992.

Kristeva, Julia. *Strangers to Ourselves*. Translated by Leon S. Roudiez. New York: Columbia University Press, 1994.

Laqueur, Walter, and Judith Tydor Baumel, ed. *The Holocaust Encyclopedia*. New Haven: Yale University Press, 2001.

Lasker, Daniel J. *Jewish Philosophical Polemics against Christianity in the Middle Ages*. New York: Ktav, 1977.

———. "The Karaite as Other" [Hebrew]. *Pe'amim* 89 (fall 2001): 97–106.

Leaman, Oliver. *Evil and Suffering in Jewish Philosophy*. Cambridge: Cambridge University Press, 1995.

Lessing, Theodor. *Der jüdische Selbsthaß*. Debatte 5. Munich: Matthes und Seitz, 1984.

Levinas, Emmanuel. *Difficult Freedom: Essays on Judaism*. Translated by Seán Hand. Baltimore: Johns Hopkins University Press, 1990.

———. *Entre nous: On Thinking-of-the-Other*. Translated by Michael B. Smith and Barbara Harshav. Columbia University Press, 1998.

———. *Éthique comme philosophie première*. Edited by
Jacques Rolland. Paris: Payot, 1998.

———. *Humanism of the Other*. Translated by Nidra Poller.
Urbana: University of Illinois Press, 2003.

———. *New Talmudic Readings*. Translated by Richard
Cohen. Pittsburgh: Duquesne University Press, 1999.

———. *Nine Talmudic Readings*. Translated by Annette
Aronowicz. Bloomington: Indiana University Press,
1990.

———. *Time and the Other and Additional Essays*. Translated by Richard A. Cohen. Pittsburgh: Duquesne University Press, 1987.

———. *Le visage de l'autre*. Paris: Le Seuil, 2001.

Levy, Zeev. *Otherness and Responsibility: A Study of the
Philosophy of Emmanuel Levinas*. Jerusalem: Magnes,
1997. [Hebrew.]

Loewenstein, Rudolph. *Christians and Jews: A Psychoana-
lytic Study*. Translated by Vera Damman. New York:
International Universities Press, 1951.

Maimonides, Moses. *Epistles of Maimonides: Crisis and
Leadership*. Edited and translated by Abraham
Halkin. Philadelphia: Jewish Publication Society,
1993.

———. *The Guide of the Perplexed*. Edited by Julius
Guttmann. Translated by Chaim Rebin. Indianapolis:
Hackett, 1995.

Massad, Joseph. "Zionism's Internal Others: Israel and the
Oriental Jews." *Journal of Palestine Studies* 25/4 (sum-
mer 1996): 53–68.

Melamed, Abraham. *The Black as "Other" in the History
of Jewish Culture*. Tel Aviv: Zmora-Bitan, 2002. [He-
brew.]

Mendes-Flohr, Paul. *German Jews: A Dual Identity*. New
Haven: Yale University Press, 1999.

Mopsik, Charles. *Le Sexe des âmes: Aléas de la différence
sexuelle dans la Cabale*. Paris and Tel Aviv: L'Eclat,
2003.

Moragh, Gilead. "The Arab as 'Other' in Israeli Fiction."
   Middle East Review 22/1 (fall 1989): 35–40.

Moseley, Marcus. "Jewish Autobiography in Eastern Europe: The Pre-History of a Literary Genre." PhD diss.,
   Trinity College, Dublin, 1990.

Neusner, Jacob and Ernest S. Frerichs, ed. *"To See Ourselves as Others See Us": Christians, Jews, "Others" in
   Late Antiquity*. Chico, Calif.: Scholars Press, 1985.

Nochlin, Linda, and Tarmar Garb, ed. *The Jew in the Text:
   Modernity and the Construction of Identity*. London:
   Thames and Hudson, 1995.

Osier, Jean-Pierre. *D'Uriel de Costa à Spinoza*. Paris: Berg
   International, 1983.

———. *L'Évangile du ghetto, ou comment les Juifs racontaient Jésus*. Paris: Berg International, 1984.

Pardès 7 (1988). Special issue: Israël face aux nations: Figures juives d'autrui.

Pines, Shlomo. *Studies in the History of Jewish Thought*.
   Edited by Warren Zev Halvey and Moshe Idel.
   Jerusalem: Magnes, 1997.

Piterberg, Gabriel. "Domestic Orientalism: The Representation of 'Oriental' Jews in Zionist/Israeli Historiography." *British Journal of Middle Eastern Studies* 23
   (1996): 125–145.

Raz-Krakotzkin, Amnon. "Exile in Sovereignty: For a Critique of the 'Negation of the Exile' in Israeli Culture"
   [Hebrew]. *Teoria u-vikoret* 4 (fall 1993): 23–55 and 5
   (1994): 113–132.

Révah, I. S. *Des Marranes à Spinoza*. Paris: Vrin, 1995.

Rosenzweig, Franz. *The Star of Redemption*. Translated by
   William W. Hallo. Boston: Beacon Press, 1971.

Rotschild, Fritz A. *Jewish Perspectives on Christianity: Leo
   Baeck, Franz Rosenzweig, Will Herberg and Abraham
   J. Heschel*. New York: Continuum, 1996.

Said, Edward W. *Orientalism*. New York: Pantheon Books,
   1978.

Sartre, Jean-Paul. *Portrait of the Anti-Semite*. Translated by

Erik de Mauny. London: Secker and Warburg, Lindsay Drummond, 1948.

Schorsch, Ismar. "The Myth of Sephardic Supremacy." *Leo Baeck Institute Year Book* 34 (1989): 47–66.

Schroeter, Daniel J. "Orientalism and the Jews of the Mediterranean." *Journal of Mediterranean Studies* 4/2 (1994): 183–196.

Segev, Tom. *The First Israelis, 1949.* New York: Free Press, 1986.

Shohat, Ella. *Israeli Cinema.* Austin: University of Texas, 1989.

Silberstein, Laurence J., ed. *Mapping Jewish Identities.* New York: New York University Press, 2000.

Silberstein, Laurence J., and Robert L. Cohn, ed. *The Other in Jewish Thought and History: Constructions of Jewish Culture and Identity.* New York: New York University Press, 1994.

Smooha, Sammy. *Arabs and Jews in Israel.* Boulder: Westview Press, 1989–1992.

Swirski, Shlomo. *Israel: The Oriental Majority.* Translated by Barbara Swirski. Atlantic Highlands: Zed Books, 1989.

Twersky, Isadore. *Introduction to the Code of Maimonides (Mishneh Torah).* New Haven: Yale University Press, 1980.

Vajda, Georges. *L'Amour de Dieu dans la théologie juive du Moyen Âge.* Paris: Vrin, 1957.

Wachtel, Nathau. *La Foi du Souvenir: Labyrinthes marranes.* Paris: Seuil, 2001.

Yerushalmi, Yosef Hayim. *From Spanish Court to Italian Ghetto. Isaac Cardoso: A Study In Seventeenth-Century Marranism and Jewish Apologetics.* New York: Columbia University Press, 1981.

——. *Sefardica: Essais sur l'histoire des Juifs, des marranes et des nouveaux-chrétiens d'origine hispano-portugaise.* Translated by Cyril Aslanoff et al. Paris: Chandeigne, 1998.

Yovel, Yirmiyahu. *La nouvelle altérité: Dualités marranes des premières générations.* Translated by Carine Brenner et al. Paris: Centre Alberto Benveniste, 2002.

——. *Spinoza and Other Heretics.* 2 vols. Princeton: Princeton University Press, 1989–1991.